STEEL TRADING 4.0

• FROM TRUST TO TRANSFORMATION •

STEEL 4.0 TRADING

• FROM TRUST TO TRANSFORMATION •

ASHISH AGARWAL

Available on amazonkindle

Worldwide Published by

Pendown Press
PREMIUM BUSINESS PUBLISHER

PENDOWN PRESS LLP
An ISO 9001 & ISO 14001 Certified Co.,
Regd. Office: 3767A, Kanhaiya Nagar,
Tri Nagar, Delhi-110035
Ph.: 8130886000, 9650072927
E-mail: info@pendownpress.com
Branch Office: 1A/2A, 20, Hari Sadan, Ansari Road,
Daryaganj, New Delhi-110002
Ph.: 011-45794768
Website: PendownPress.com

Edition: 2026
Price: ₹ 499
ISBN: 978-93-7217-854-8

Layout and Cover Designed by Pendown Graphics Team

Table of Contents

Foreword

Who When I look back on our family's journey in the steel industry, one word that comes to my mind is honesty.

Honesty was the foundation of our business.

It was honesty that carried us through challenges. And it is honesty that I see shining in my son, Ashish.

From a very young age, he has shown a rare clarity and a vision that business is not just about making profits, but about expanding with purpose. Expansion not just of factories, but of trust, of opportunities, and of lives touched by it.

Every time our company grew, I saw him asking one simple question:

"How can this growth benefit not only us, but also our traders, agents, partners, and the team?"

This mindset of giving more business and creating more opportunities for all the stakeholders is what makes him different.

I believe this book is an extension of that same vision. It is not written only for traders to learn strategies, but for them to feel encouraged, supported, and as a reminder that long-term growth is possible when you combine systems with sincerity.

As a father, I feel proud. As a mentor, I feel hopeful. And as someone who has walked this path before, I feel confident that the lessons shared here will guide many of you.

May this book inspire you to think bigger, act wiser, and build with honesty for everyone in the industry.

~Mr. Parmanand Agarwal

Introduction: Why Steel Trading 4.0?

Rajesh slammed his Nokia shut after the fifteenth call that morning. It was 2005, and he had just spent three hours trying to lock in a 5,000-ton steel deal with suppliers across Mumbai, Kolkata, and Dubai.

- All he had with him then was his phonebook, a calculator, and twenty years of relationship-building that taught him which voices to trust on crackling international calls.
- His son Arjun now runs the same company, closes deals worth double that amount during his morning coffee, with a smartphone in hand, global prices streaming live on his computer, supplier credentials verified instantly, and contracts executed digitally.

What changed?

The way steel trading is done!

It has changed more in the last 10–15 years than in the many decades before.

Let's take a look at how it changed over the years-

Steel Trading 1.0 was built on physical relationships and regional markets. Deals happened face-to-face, information traveled through personal networks, and trust was earned over decades within local markets.

Steel Trading 2.0 brought the telecommunications revolution. Fax machines, mobile phones, and early internet enabled global connections, but deals were still sealed on phone calls, with reputation carrying more weight than paperwork.

Steel Trading 3.0 introduced digital integration. Real-time pricing, online platforms, and digital contracts emerged, though traditional relationship-based methods often clashed with new technology.

Now we're in Steel Trading 4.0, where digital transparency combines with human trust. Today, information is at everyone's fingertips. Prices, supply, demand, even trader backgrounds, everything is available at a click or tap.

The system has become far more transparent, and with more liquidity in the market, the margin for error is shrinking.

- **In this new environment, one thing is very clear:** those who stay honest, keep their communication upfront, and build system-driven trading practices will always profit more than those who try to chase shortcuts.
- **Unfortunately, many traders are still stuck in outdated practices,** believing they can hide the truth, thinking the other side "won't know." But the reality is, everyone knows everything. Miscommunication, over-promises, and shortcuts no longer work. Clear-cut dealing is the only way forward.

But you know what I find most interesting about all this?

It's not the technology or apps that matter the most, but the relationships.

Actually, they matter more now. Markets go up and down. New systems keep coming. But people still want to do business with people they trust.

That's why, as we step into **Steel Trading 4.0,** I believe the true revolution is a mix of **digital transparency + long-term human trust.**

This book is my attempt to guide today's steel traders to grow faster, avoid outdated mistakes, and build a future where profits are stable and relationships are strong.

A Heartfelt Note

Every second-generation entrepreneur faces a hidden test:

You inherit not just a business from your father, but also its **habits, its systems (or the lack of them), and the expectations that "you will handle everything."**

When I started, this was exactly my reality. The plant was running, but at a loss. I remember one particular day when I walked across the factory floor, looked at the numbers, and asked myself: Why are we losing money despite all this hard work?

I gathered everyone, questioned every detail, finally came to a conclusion, and did something that even I wasn't prepared for.

I shut the plant down. And restarted it from scratch.

Why?

Because I realized the biggest problem wasn't the machines or the market.

It was that people were doing their jobs, but nobody was thinking about the bigger picture.

- Purchases were happening, but no one felt responsible for the costs.
- Sales were being done, but no one owned the targets.
- Production was rolling, but no one was accountable for efficiency.

For years, I carried the entire weight on my own shoulders. I was the buyer, seller, accountant, strategist, all in one. And because of this, for almost 14 years, we could not expand.

But slowly and painfully, I learned to shift responsibility from the owner to the doer. From "I will handle it" to "you can do it." And once that trust was built, things started changing.

We went from being one of the **slowest to expand in the industry** to being among the **fastest to grow.**

The Shift: From Basics to Innovation

The changes that happened were enormous, but the result was just the outer layer. Now, let's try to go deeper into the layers of the journey.

When I entered the steel trading industry, the market looked very different.

Knowledge was limited, access to data was restricted, and deals happened on trust, phone calls, and reputation.

It was a **"one-man show"** style of working.

I personally handled everything, from signing cheques, meeting every supplier, visiting every buyer, to following up on payments, and even handling logistics. At that time, it felt natural.

After all, this was how the previous generation had built businesses.

But as the market grew bigger, I realized one thing very clearly: **You either evolve or you get left behind.**

The Turning Point

There came a moment when I personally realized that the old style would no longer work.

The industry was expanding fast, more competitors were coming in, information was moving faster than ever, and suddenly, trying to do everything myself was actually hurting the business.

- Customers wanted quicker responses.
- Suppliers needed faster decisions.
- Markets were moving while I was stuck in meetings or traveling between cities.

One person simply couldn't keep up with all of this anymore.

That's when I understood that building systems, using technology, and having a strong team was no longer a choice, but the only way to grow the business.

That's when I started freeing my time for strategy, vision & growth, and started building a team that could handle operations better than I could alone.

This was the real shift, from survival trading to system-driven, innovation-led growth.

Our Innovation Journey

One of the biggest shifts in my company came when we separated "follow-up work" from leadership work.

Earlier, both the MD and salespersons were drowning in small tasks:

- Chasing payments
- Checking dispatches
- Calling for follow-ups

But we all know that the real value of a salesperson is in building relationships, meeting customers, and closing bigger deals.

So we created a **dedicated CRM team** to handle routine follow-ups. The result was this-

- ✅ Sales teams got more face time with clients.
- ✅ Relationships deepened.
- ✅ Efficiency multiplied across departments.

This simple shift increased productivity multi-fold and gave us the confidence to scale faster.

The Role of Young Blood

I've seen how today's youngsters outperform many mid-aged traders. Because they are fast to grasp new ideas, take quick decisions, and don't let ego hold them back.

They travel, they meet people, and they adopt innovations without fear. That's why they are reshaping the face of steel trading.

So, Why This Book?

Somewhere along the way, I realized my story is not just mine.

Thousands of steel traders face the same struggles:

- Carrying everything alone.
- Fearing delegation.
- Stuck between old methods and new realities.

This book is my way of saying: you are not alone.

I want to communicate better with my agents, my traders, my peers. I want to share the lessons that took me years to learn so that others can save time, avoid mistakes, and find their own growth path faster.

And honestly, I also want to hear their stories back. Because trading means building relationships, going through struggles together, and growing as a team.

Who Is This Book For?

This book is written for **steel traders,** especially those standing at the crossroads of tradition and transformation.

The Transformation I Hope For

When you finish this book, I want you to feel three things:

1. **Relief** that the problems you face are real and solvable.

2. **Clarity** on how honesty, systems, and relationships make business easier.
3. **Confidence** that profits are possible not just with me, but with any supplier, manufacturer, or partner, if the fundamentals are right.

Most of all, I want you to walk away with a new belief:

That steel trading in today's world is not about survival; it is about 2x growth with innovation.

As I share my journey, I am reminded of a timeless doha by Kabir:

"साईं इतना दीजिए, जामें कुटुंब समाय।
मैं भी भूखा न रहूँ, साधु न भूखा जाय॥"

(Give me just enough, Lord, that I can care for my family

And still have something left to serve others.)

This captures the very spirit of steel trading today.

- We are not in business just to accumulate wealth.
- We are here to create value, to serve our stakeholders, to build trust that outlives profits and losses.

For me, relationships have always mattered more than short-term gains. And that is the essence of Steel Trading 4.0: trading with honesty, innovation, and responsibility, so that together, we can all grow faster and stronger.

Sincerely yours

Ashish Agarwal
Founder, BS Group

PART 1

THE NEW REALITY OF STEEL TRADING

CHAPTER 1

Steel Trading Then (The Old Paradigm)

When I first stepped into the steel trade, deals were done in a very simple way. It needed just a phone call, a word, and it was done. If someone said, "*Material kal subah load ho jayega,*" (The material will be loaded tomorrow), you knew it would happen.

The real contract was never made on paper; it was based on your reputation in the market.

- People operated on trust.
- Your word carried more weight than any legal document could ever.
- Paperwork existed, but it was mostly for record-keeping.
- What mattered was whether traders believed you would deliver what you promised.

In short, reputation mattered much more than any written or signed contract.

The Shift

When we look at today's reality, it looks completely different.

- People no longer deal based on just reputation or a call.

- ➢ Corporate buyers demand more, like POs, GST compliance, and digital invoices, before they even discuss prices.
- ➢ Systems have replaced handshakes or words.
- ➢ Processes have replaced personal guarantees and reputation in the market.

But here's what's still interesting: in traditional trading circles, one phone call still closes deals like earlier.

So we're living in this unique time where both worlds exist side by side. Some trades happen with full documentation and digital workflows, while others still run on the old foundation of trust and relationships.

This blend of old and new is what defines today's steel trading landscape.

The Role of Credit

Credit was the oxygen of trading; in other words, "Udhār pe bikta tha maal" (Material was sold on credit).

The entire industry ran on extended payment cycles. Suppliers would deliver material and wait 60, 90, sometimes even 120 days to get paid. Buyers expected this. It was the standard way business worked.

The unspoken rule was simple: if you wanted to sell steel, you had to be willing to wait for your money.

When I started trading TMTs, people told me, "Credit ke bina koi nahi lega" (No one will buy unless you extend credit). The assumption was that without offering extended payment terms like others were doing in the industry, we'd have no customers.

But even then, we took a different path.

Instead of competing on credit terms, we decided to compete on reliability.

We built a policy of honest dealings:

- Standard weight,
- Proper stacking and packaging,
- And delivering exactly what we promised, whether in chemical composition or physical properties.

Slowly, buyers realized we delivered what we said. Trust replaced the need for credit, and soon they began paying us on a loading-payment basis.

A Story from the Old Days

In my father's time, traders often worked with just 2–3 buyers for decades. Profit or loss didn't matter.

"Apna aadmi hai" (He is a part of our community) was enough to continue.

I remember, once, a buyer stayed with us even when our prices were slightly higher. He said:

"Ashish ji, rate mein ek-do rupaye ka fark ho sakta hai. Lekin bharosa, woh priceless hai."

(Ashish ji, the rate may vary by a rupee or two, but trust is priceless.)

That was how old trading worked. Back then, steel traders cared more about keeping long-term relationships than making short-term profits. They knew that a trusted relationship would bring business for years, even if individual deals weren't always the most profitable.

You built relationships and kept them strong through good times and bad times.

But here's the big question: Can this old way of doing business still work today?

In a world where everything is digital, prices are transparent, and competition is fierce, do these deep personal relationships still have the same value?

Or do we need to find new ways to build trust while also staying competitive in the modern market?

Why Old Methods Aren't Enough Today

The old ways had their charm, but they also came with shortcomings. Deals often ran on assumptions. If one party said "*yeh rate sahi hai*" (This rate is right) or "yeh weight theek hai," (This weight is perfect), the other side had no option but to accept.

This led to problems:

- **Defaults:** Payments delayed for months, sometimes never recovered
- **Delays:** Material stuck due to miscommunication or one agent holding the file

- **Frauds:** Faulty weights, compromised quality, and manipulated documents
- **Dependency:** The entire business hanging on one middleman

I remember having an agent whom I trusted completely, like a family member. Over time, I realized he wasn't always working in my best interest. The trust broke, and that mistake taught me that you cannot build a long-term business on half-truths or blind reliance.

Today, things have changed completely.

You need clear communication, proper documentation, and honest dealing. I've watched many traders struggle because they refused to change. They kept thinking that just phone calls and old relationships would be enough. Meanwhile, other traders who started using proper systems and being more transparent took over their business.

Why? Because now everyone knows everything. Buyers can check rates from multiple suppliers instantly. They can track their orders online. They can verify everything. You can't hide anything anymore, and honestly, you shouldn't even try.

The New Reality of Steel Trading

Last month, I got to hear about a contractor who rejected a ₹50 lakh steel order because the supplier couldn't provide digital tracking. Ten years ago, that same contractor would have bought steel based on a phone call and a promise.

Today, the ground reality is different. Organized builders, developers, and contractors demand far more because the stakes are higher.

Certification & Standards

Builders now insist on standardized TMT products, not underweight material. Every major project requires lab reports, test certificates, and ISI compliance. Why? Because if the steel in a building fails, the whole building can collapse, and the entire structure is at risk.

Digital Tracking & Transparency

Gone are the days when a truck's location was a mystery. Today, GPS-enabled tracking ensures that material is traceable from source to site. In our units, even incoming raw material is tracked digitally to eliminate doubts of pilferage or tampering.

Compliance as a Growth Driver

Earlier, people used to be afraid of compliance. Now it helps you grow your business. Look at GST: when real-time billing and e-invoicing became mandatory, most businesses had to operate properly.

The grey market became smaller, and honest businesses got more opportunities. In short, having a clean record opens doors to bigger contracts, institutional buyers, and bank support.

Rise of Digital Systems

Where ledgers were once written by hand, now even small traders use ERP, CRMs, and e-invoicing in their business dealings. I met two brothers running a ₹100 crore business with just their laptops and no employees. Their secret was nothing but that they managed everything through digital systems.

The New Mindset

All this shows a clear shift: Success in steel trading today depends on how reliable and transparent you are, not just how much steel you sell. Today, buyers want both:

- Steel that they can trust
- Processes they can verify

Traders who don't adapt to these changes are losing business. In the era of Steel trading 4.0, having good systems and being honest is what builds your reputation.

How the BS Group Adapted

At BS Group, this transition happened organically:

- As manpower increased, we added new rooms and facilities
- As transactions grew, we replaced paperwork with ERP systems
- To eliminate disputes, we installed an automatic weighbridge
- We evolved IT and CRM teams as per the needs that changed

We didn't plan all of this from the beginning. We simply solved problems as they came up. When we faced a challenge, we found a way to fix it. In short, Necessity became the mother of invention.

My Advice to Young Traders

If I had to give one piece of advice, it would be this:

Be honest. Communicate openly.

Spend time in the market. Learn deeply.

In the beginning, you may get less work because you're not taking any shortcuts. But over time, people will trust you, respect you, and prefer to deal with you. And in business, trust is the only currency that multiplies with use.

CHAPTER 2

The Trust Factor

Why Trust > Price

In steel trading, numbers matter, be it in terms of price, quality, or tonnage. But there's one factor that outweighs them all: trust.

As I often say, if trust is missing, even the best price or highest quality won't matter. Because trust is the human foundation of business. Without it, every deal feels uncertain, and no matter how attractive the rate is, doubts creep in: "Will the material arrive on time? Will the weight be correct? Will the commitment hold?"

And doubts kill growth.

We know that steel trading is not as simple as selling a t-shirt or a gadget. A single truck of steel can decide the fate of an entire project. If one delivery fails, the site may shut down. If one batch is underweight, the contractor loses money. If one invoice is unclear, the builder loses confidence.

So what are buyers really buying? Not just steel rods. They are buying reliability and peace of mind.

The Real Cost of Broken Trust

A trader who delivers late, hides facts, or plays games with weight may win a deal today, but will lose the market trust tomorrow. Undercutting prices may help in the short term. Yes, you may get a few orders because you were the cheapest. But this approach always collapses. Margins shrink, quality suffers, and eventually, buyers realize that “cheap” came at too high a cost.

One of the most common questions I hear is:

“Why would a buyer pay a higher rate when someone else is offering cheaper?”

The answer is simple: **certainty.**

When a broker invests ₹10, 20, or even 50 lakh in steel, they’re putting a lot on the line. And no broker will risk that amount with someone uncertain, even if the price is lower. They look for something bigger than price; they look for assurance.

The Power of Trust

Take the example of Tata. Their products are not always the cheapest. In fact, sometimes they are more expensive than others. Yet, buyers line up for Tata Steel because of one thing: assurance. They know that their money, their project, and their reputation are safe when the name Tata is involved.

That is the power of trust. It not only brings business, but it also builds a brand. And once your name becomes synonymous with trust, you no longer have to fight in price wars. Buyers choose you because of confidence, not cost.

One buyer once explained it beautifully: “Ashish ji, dealing with you is like putting money in the bank. I know that in any situation, even if there is a problem, I will either get my material or my money back.”

That confidence is priceless. Over the years, I’ve seen buyers repeatedly choose us even when our rate was slightly higher. Because markets talk. Word spreads. And the market always knows who is genuine and who keeps their commitments.

A trader who is upfront, transparent, and dependable may not always be the cheapest, but they will always be the first choice. Because in the long run, trust is cheaper than price. It saves buyers the hidden costs of disputes, delays, and rework. And it saves traders the endless cycle of chasing new customers.

Trust compounds like interest. The more consistently you honor it, the more valuable it becomes, far beyond what price alone can achieve.

Market Has Its Own Memory

You know what’s fascinating about our industry?

The market itself acts like a judge.

Traders think they can get away with taking shortcuts, but the truth always comes out. A wrong weight here, a delayed truck there, or a broken promise, all of it spreads in the market faster than WhatsApp messages.

But when you consistently stand by your word, refund when required, and never let a buyer’s trust break, the market remembers that too. That reputation pulls business toward you, sometimes even at higher prices.

Because in the end, for a broker or developer, it's not about saving ₹100 per tonne. It's about sleeping peacefully, knowing their money is safe.

Trust is a Two-Way Street

You know, when people talk about trust in steel trading, they usually focus on quality or delivering on time. But for me, trust goes much deeper than that; it's really about both parties taking responsibility for their part of the deal.

When a deal is finalized, whether it is for 100 tonnes or 1,000 tonnes, the terms should remain steady. The rate, the quantity, the commitment: none of these should change midway. Because the moment they do, trust breaks.

But trust is not one-sided. It is not only about the supplier delivering on time, but also about the trader lifting the material on time.

When delays happen on the supplier's end, they should acknowledge them openly and work to fix them. Similarly, when delays happen on the buyer's end, everyone expects the same honesty and accountability. This mutual respect for taking ownership is what keeps relationships strong.

What I've come to understand over the years is that trust isn't really about being perfect or never making mistakes. In business, errors are going to happen; that's just reality.

What actually matters is whether both sides are willing to step up and be accountable when something goes wrong. That willingness to take responsibility, that's what trust really means.

Transparency builds trust

One of the strongest examples of how *transparency builds trust* in steel trading comes from our automatic weighbridge system.

In the past, weighing was often a grey area. Buyers would always wonder, "*Is the scale showing the true weight, or has someone tampered with it?*" Even a 10–20 kg difference per truck could add up to big losses over time. And unfortunately, in many places, manipulation of weights was not uncommon.

To solve this, we have also been using a manless automatic weighbridge. Here, there is no manual intervention. The truck drives in, the system records the exact weight digitally, and the report is generated instantly. No staff member can interfere; no one can adjust numbers, it is the same for everyone.

I still remember the first reaction of a buyer when he saw it in action. He stepped out of his car, looked at the digital display, and after a pause, said: ***"Ashish ji, ab toh bharosa double ho gaya."*** (Ashish ji, now our faith has doubled) For him, seeing those numbers meant his money was safe. He knew there was no hidden hand tilting the scale in anyone's favor.

This small shift changed the way people saw our company. Buyers who once hesitated to make large advance payments became more confident. They knew that what we promised was exactly what we delivered, no more, no less.

What did I learn from this?

Trust is not built by big speeches; it is built by small systems.

One transparent process can do more for relationships than a hundred meetings. And once buyers feel safe with you, they will choose you again and again, even if the rate is not the lowest in the market.

Transparency as a Growth Driver

You know, when people think about transparency, they often focus on systems like weighbridges and ERPs. But honestly, transparency starts much earlier than that. It begins with how you treat someone the very first time they walk through your door.

When a new client approaches us, the first thing we do is invite them to visit our factory. There is no better proof than letting them see with their own eyes how the plant runs, the processes, the weighbridge, or the material quality. When the doors are open, doubts begin to disappear.

Secondly, we encourage them to speak directly with our old clients. Testimonials are powerful, but hearing a genuine experience from someone who has already worked with us carries much more weight. It gives them real insights into what they can expect.

Finally, I believe in direct conversation with the owner. When I personally speak to a buyer, I make sure they feel heard. I tell them:

"Whatever happens, you will always get a proper response from us. Even if there is an issue, we will face it together."

That direct assurance builds confidence. Because real transparency means being available, open, and accountable right from that very first conversation. It's not just about the reports you show or the digital systems you have; it's about how you make someone feel when they're deciding whether to trust you.

In the end, for a new client, transparency is not what you say, but it is what you allow them to see, feel, and verify for themselves.

Transparency: A Cost Today, A Premium Tomorrow

Being transparent isn't always the easiest path. Sometimes it means investing more to ensure you deliver exactly what you promise.

I remember when we started supplying ferro-silico-manganese. We made a commitment to deliver exactly a 60 by 4 specification, not the minimum acceptable standard, but the exact specification our customers expected.

At first, this approach required a higher investment. We were spending ₹500 to ₹1,000 more per tonne on better raw materials and more precise processes to consistently hit that exact specification. We could have aimed for just meeting minimum requirements, but we wanted to exceed expectations.

But something interesting happened over time. Buyers started recognizing the consistency. They knew that with us, what was promised was exactly what was delivered - no surprises, no variations.

Today, instead of that extra investment being a cost, we actually earn a premium in the market for maintaining that standard. Why? Because once trust is built around consistency, people don't just compare you on price. They compare you on reliability and peace of mind.

The lesson I learned: Investing more to deliver exactly what you promise may cost more initially, but it creates value that goes far beyond the extra expense. It builds genuine trust.

How Transparency Fuels 2x Growth

If I had to point to one factor that doubled our growth in recent years, it would be transparency.

Because of transparency, we can sell **everything we produce.** Nothing sits idle, nothing needs pushing. Buyers know exactly what they are getting, the right weight, the right quality, the right documentation. This confidence removes hesitation from their side.

The result

- **Faster Orders:** Clients don't waste time double-checking. They confirm quickly because they trust the process.
- **Repeat Clients:** Once someone experiences honest dealing, they come back again and again.

- **Larger Contracts:** Builders and developers who start small eventually give us bigger volumes because they know there will be no surprises.

In the last five years, this cycle of trust → demand → production has inspired us to increase our production capacity continuously.

Transparency has not only built our reputation; it has pushed us to grow, scale, and serve bigger projects with confidence.

In short, transparency doesn't just keep relationships smooth; it accelerates growth, creates demand, and multiplies opportunities.

My Advice to Young Traders

One of the biggest mistakes I see traders making is failing to honor commitments. They delay, renegotiate, or back out of deals that don't seem profitable at first instance. In the short term, they think they saved money, but in the long term, they lose something far more valuable, i.e., trust.

If a young trader asked me,

"Should I cut my price or build my trust?"

My answer is simple: Always build your trust.

Price fluctuates. Margins rise and fall. But trust gives peace of mind to both the customer and you. And that's priceless.

CHAPTER 3

Market Challenges Every Trader Faces

Every day in steel trading brings new challenges that can test your business. Credit issues, payment delays, quality disputes, transportation problems, and regulatory changes, each one can disrupt your operations if you're not prepared.

But if I had to pick the biggest challenge that tests every trader, it's market volatility.

In our industry, prices can fluctuate overnight. A sudden swing can completely change the math of a deal. I've seen many traders cancel their deals, delay picking up material, or simply disappear when market prices change. They use market changes as an excuse to break their promises.

But I believe differently. A deal is a deal. If I've committed at a rate, I will honor it, regardless of whether the market goes up or down.

Of course, volatility does test relationships. With suppliers, the rules have become tighter - most now ask us to complete lifting within 7 to 10 days. Even then, because of the trust we've built, they give us breathing space to close deals without breaking commitments.

With buyers, it's mixed. Most trusted buyers still honor their deals. But if there are any delays, some cancel the deals outright.

To overcome this situation, over time, we built a strategy that helped us and our clients navigate this challenge.

We introduced a **One Rate Policy;** whatever rate we open on a given day remains fixed for all clients that day, no matter how the market moves. Even if the market rises, we don't increase the price for that day's committed orders.

This policy is uncommon in our industry, but it has worked wonders. Clients know exactly what to expect; they don't feel cheated, and most importantly, they feel secure that our word is stronger than market volatility.

That is how trust is built, and that is why price will always remain secondary.

Payment Delays

In steel trading, deals don't end at dispatch. They end when the payment comes in, and sometimes, that's where the real test begins.

The longest I've waited to get my money back was more than two months. Those sixty days taught me one of the hardest lessons in trading: Even good names in the market need due diligence.

It's easy to assume that a reputable company or a long-term partner will always pay on time. But assumptions are dangerous. That experience showed me that even trusted relationships must be backed by checks, balances, and systems.

Now, we follow a clear principle:

- **Selective credit only** we extend credit to a very limited set of buyers.
- **Due diligence every time,** no matter how good a buyer's reputation is, our team conducts background checks before approving large exposures.
- **Dedicated monitoring,** a separate team keeps an eye on buyers' financial behavior and ensures risks don't pile up unnoticed.

The Cost of Delays

Payment delays directly hurt growth. Without timely inflows, no business can expand. Every late payment adds to our interest cost, squeezes our cash flow, and slows down the ability to seize new opportunities

To counter this, we've built a layered system:

- **CRM Follow-up:** After seven days of delay, our CRM team immediately calls the buyer.
- **Escalation:** If the delay stretches to ten days, the Head of Department is informed.
- **Action:** No fresh material is dispatched to that party until the pending payment is cleared.

This structured approach not only protects us from defaults but also sends a clear message to buyers: transparency and timeliness go both ways.

In trading, credit may drive volume, but discipline drives survival. That lesson from my longest delay remains one of my strongest principles.

Supply Chain Disruptions: The Unseen Challenge

Every trader dreams of smooth operations, but the reality is that supply chains are fragile.

I still remember a season when iron from Barbil faced major transportation issues. Trucks were stuck, movement was delayed, and our entire supply chain management felt the heat.

For a business where time is money, even a few days of delay can shake trust and profitability. That incident taught us a **key lesson to always keep a buffer stock.**

Today, we ensure that seasonal disruptions or transport bottlenecks don't paralyze operations. A little preparedness protects both our business and our clients.

Turning Crisis into Trust

But disruptions don't always have to end in loss. Sometimes, they can become opportunities to build stronger trust.

There was a time when one of our suppliers couldn't supply the material on time. They came back to us and said, "We can give you the material, but only at a higher price. In return, you'll get better quality."

We could have refused, argued, or tried to force old terms. But instead, we accepted. Because business is about relationships, not just rates.

By giving the supplier a chance to earn in that situation, we ensured our own supply continued, and our clients were not left stranded. It became a win-win.

In trading, sometimes the balance of power shifts; at times, the supplier is stronger, at times, we are. What matters is how you handle those moments. If you approach them with fairness, communication, and flexibility, every crisis becomes a chance to deepen mutual respect.

Key lesson: Supply chain disruptions are inevitable. But how you respond, by panicking or by partnering, decides whether you lose business or gain trust.

Competing with Larger Players

One of the biggest challenges in our industry comes from competing with larger, branded players.

They have one clear advantage: pricing power.

Big players often offer heavy discounts that smaller or midsize traders cannot match. And in B2B steel trading, unlike consumer markets, brand value doesn't carry the same weight, because most products, whether from a small or big company, are almost equal in quality.

So, when buyers get swayed only by lower prices, it becomes a tough battleground. But here's what we've learned: **trust and consistency beat price wars.**

Why Buyers Still Choose Us

Despite the advantage of big brands, many of our buyers continue to work with us, often giving us at least 50% of their business.

Because they know:

- Our chemical composition is consistent.
- Our quality standards are never compromised.
- Our word is as strong as our delivery.

When customers buy from us, they're buying steel they can count on.

One furnace owner once told me,

"Price ek-do rupaye kam zyada ho sakti hai, par agar maal waqt par na mile toh hamara pura plant ruk jaata hai. Hum unhi se kharidenge jo samajhte hain ki hamara dard kya hai."

(The price may be one or two rupees higher or lower, but if the material doesn't arrive on time, our entire plant comes to a halt. We will buy only from those who understand what our pain is.)

That's the real edge smaller or midsize players can hold: we're closer to the ground, quicker to respond, and more empathetic to client needs.

Differentiation Despite Limited Scale

Smaller traders can actually turn scale into strength. While large players push bulk volumes and chase margins, smaller traders often operate with leaner teams and faster responsiveness. Many work on commission, which makes them sharper and more focused on customer satisfaction.

Bigger traders are still important because they can lift large volumes, but the value of smaller traders lies in their flexibility, personal connections, and service.

Service Over Price

In the end, **timely supply and understanding the buyer's pain points matter more than discounts.**

For example, when sponge iron demand suddenly spiked, bigger companies with lower prices couldn't deliver on time. Buyers turned to us because we understood their urgency. By ensuring on-time delivery, we helped them cut inventory costs and keep their furnaces running.

That is the lesson every trader should remember: price may win the deal, but service wins the relationship.

Strategy Over Luck: A Turning Point

Every business faces moments where survival depends not on luck, but on the ability to make the right strategic move.

For us, one such turning point came in 2013–14. Margins had collapsed, and our conversion unit was bleeding losses. It felt like every decision carried extra weight because the future of the company depended on it.

At that time, a company called Jindal Steel & Power Ltd. approached us. They proposed a conversion deal; we would supply sponge iron, and they would provide finished material in return.

Traditionally, we had never done such arrangements. It was outside our comfort zone. But desperate times demand a decisive strategy. Instead of waiting for things to turn around, I immediately said yes.

For the next 2–3 months, I personally visited their offices, followed up on payments, and ensured the relationship worked smoothly. It wasn't easy, but that one strategic decision helped us cross the bridge of losses during one of the toughest periods in our journey.

The lesson was clear: In steel trading, survival doesn't come from waiting for luck. It comes from making bold, timely, and sometimes unconventional strategic choices.

Advice for Today's Traders

If I had to give just one piece of advice to a trader starting today, it would be this:

Focus on consistency.

Growth in this industry rarely happens overnight.

It builds slowly, but surely, on the back of consistent effort and honest work.

I'll give you an example. Years ago, a customer started working with us. In the beginning, he was handling just one or two trucks. Most people would dismiss such a small start. But he stayed consistent, month after month, year after year.

Today, he trades over 2,000 tons of sponge iron every month. That is the power of persistence.

And that's the real secret:

Steel trading is not a difficult business if you commit to consistency and honesty. Small beginnings can grow into extraordinary outcomes when trust and perseverance are your foundation.

PART 2

THE 2X GROWTH FRAMEWORK FOR STEEL TRADERS

CHAPTER 4

Introducing F.A.S.T. The System Behind 2x Growth

Most traders think business growth comes from working harder - making more calls, visiting more clients, handling more deals. But working harder without a clear system just creates more chaos, instead of more growth.

When traders ask me, "*Ashish ji, ek hi saal mein speed kaise aayi?*" (Ashish ji, how did you succeed so much in just a year?)

I don't show them a secret price list. Because there is no secret price list that magically makes you successful.

Price lists are just numbers on paper. Every trader has access to similar rates from mills. The real difference doesn't come from what you sell, but in HOW you sell it. It's in your systems, how fast you dispatch, how reliably you deliver, how efficiently you handle operations. That's what buyers actually pay for.

So instead of showing rates, I show them a simple operating system we built: F.A.S.T.

F.A.S.T. = Frequency Availability Savings Time

F.A.S.T. is not just a slogan. It's a way of working that turns everyday trading into a repeatable, compounding engine.

These four elements form the backbone of successful steel trading because they address what customers actually care about.

- **Frequency:** When a builder calls you, they want their material delivered quickly and consistently.
- **Availability:** They need to know you have the right sizes and grades in stock.
- **Savings:** They want competitive pricing that doesn't hurt their project margins.
- **Time:** And above all, they want everything delivered exactly when promised.

Everything else, fancy brochures, big office spaces, elaborate presentations, is just noise. Customers judge you on these four fundamentals. Get them right, and loyalty follows. Get them wrong, and even the best rates won't save the relationship.

Why we needed a system (not more hustle)

For years, we tried to grow by working harder, making more calls, more visits, and doing more firefighting.

Growth came, but it was uneven.

We would have one good month followed by two slow months. Our cash would get stuck somewhere in the supply chain while trucks got delayed and buyers grew impatient. Meanwhile, our team was exhausted from constantly firefighting these problems

It was after facing all this that I realised: **hustle without a system becomes chaos.**

The interesting thing about systems we learned is that they're not restrictions on freedom, they're what create freedom. When you don't have systems, you become the bottleneck. Every decision needs you. Every problem needs you. With systems, your business can run even when you're not there.

So we mapped what actually made a difference and shifted our process across dispatch, sourcing, pricing, and cash flow, and turned those learnings into four simple, practical levers anyone can run every day.

What F.A.S.T. helps with

Have you ever wondered why some traders seem to effortlessly attract loyal customers while others chase every deal? The difference isn't in their product, it's in their operating rhythm. That rhythm comes down to mastering four core areas that every successful steel trader must get right:

- **Frequency:** Move material more often, in smaller cycles. Instead of one big delivery per month, make two smaller ones. This way, money rotates faster, customers get a consistent supply, and trust builds through repeated success.
- **Availability:** Be the trader who never says "not available." Keep the right mix of sizes and grades ready. When customers know you have stock, they stop calling competitors first.
- **Savings:** Profit hides in costs, be it in freight, wastage, or handling costs. Optimize truck loads, reduce waste, and streamline operations. Every rupee saved either increases your profit or gives you better pricing power.

- **Time:** Deliver when promised, decide quickly, and collect promptly. In construction, delays cost more than savings. Consistent on-time delivery makes you indispensable, not just another supplier.

The results

Trust, in business, works like gravity. You don't see it, but everything falls apart without it.

We saw this trust in action when we implemented F.A.S.T:

- **Dispatch certainty:** When we shifted to pre-planned, ready-to-dispatch scheduling, buyers started preferring us even at the same or slightly higher rate because their furnaces couldn't wait.
- **Stock discipline:** Keeping 60–70% SKUs ready (straight + bend) meant fewer lost orders and more impulse buys. This balance ensured availability without blocking cash flow.
- **Cost clean-up:** Combining multi-product loads from one point cut freight, loading/unloading, and idle labour. Net margins rose even when the topline was flat. This worked because freight is charged per truck, not per tonne; fill the truck completely, and the cost per tonne drops automatically.
- **Time controls:** With CRM follow-ups and a One Rate Policy (same-day uniform pricing), we reduced disputes, sped up decision-making, and increased reorders. One rate eliminated confusion and built trust with buyers, knowing they're getting fair treatment.

Across five years, the compounding looked like this:

Higher repeat rate → faster rotations → stronger cash position → better raw-material buying → more reliability → bigger contracts.

There were no shortcuts or tricks involved. It was simply about building reliable systems and dealing with people honestly.

Let's talk about Frequency in the next chapter in detail!

CHAPTER 5

Why Frequency is the First Pillar

If trading is an engine, cash rotation is the fuel. And frequency is what makes money move faster and more predictably. Most traders think frequency just means speed. But it's actually about creating a steady rhythm in your business.

When your material moves more frequently, even in smaller lots, three important things happen together:

1. **Cash rotates faster**

   Shorter cycles mean your money doesn't sit idle. You buy raw material at the right time, without liquidity stress. Recently, we could take a large raw-material position because our rotations were fast; many others hesitated and lost that window.

2. **Customer flow strengthens**

   Every quick, clean delivery becomes a reason for the buyer to reorder from you. Frequency builds a routine. When customers can count on your routine, they trust you more. When they trust you more, they prefer you over competitors.

3. **Vehicle & value optimization**

   With planned loads that combine different materials, trucks run 90–100% full. This brings down freight cost per tonne, reduces wasted time, and makes your total offer more valuable, not just competitive on rates.

What "Frequency" Looks Like in Practice

Understanding frequency as a concept is one thing, but implementing it in daily operations is another. The key is turning frequency from an idea into specific, repeatable actions that your entire team can follow consistently.

These principles translate into five practical actions that any steel trader can start implementing immediately:

- **Easy and Fast Dispatches:** Plan your loads, allocate materials properly, and dispatch without last-minute confusion. This eliminates the daily chaos most traders face and builds customer confidence through predictable delivery times.
- **Right Mix Loads:** Combine different products like pipes, TMT bars, and strips in one truck. This fills trucks completely and reduces the landed cost for customers, making your offer more attractive than competitors who send separate trucks.
- **Hassle-free Offloading:** Coordinate with customers to ensure labor and equipment are ready when your trucks arrive. This prevents trucks from sitting idle at construction sites, which saves time and money for everyone involved.
- **Low Investment, Fast Rotation:** Accept smaller order quantities and stock more product varieties. This creates more frequent transactions with less money tied up in any single deal, keeping your cash flow healthy and responsive.
- **Cross-Selling and Frequent Visits:** Offer multiple products during each customer interaction and visit customers regularly throughout the month. This creates more opportunities for

orders and strengthens relationships through consistent personal contact.

Core Idea

"Jitni baar maal ghoomega, utni baar paisa ghoomega.

Aur jitna paisa ghoomega, utni tez growth hogi."

(The more times the goods circulate, the more the money circulates. And the more the money circulates, the faster the growth will be.)

Faster Dispatch = Bigger Trust

When I started, dispatch planning hardly existed.

- Orders piled up.
- Trucks got delayed.
- And buyers lost patience.

We never got the best parties or the best rates because we couldn't deliver on time.

Today, things are different. Before the buyer even asks, our trucks are ready to roll. This single habit transformed our reputation. Even if the market offers slightly cheaper rates, many buyers still prefer to work with us. Because they know their furnace cannot afford to stop.

A delay in sponge supply could shut it down, causing losses far greater than ₹100–400 per tonne. For them, certainty is worth more than saving a few rupees.

Core Idea

Dispatch speed is not just in logistics; it's in trust.

Vehicle Optimization = Profit Optimization

Every trader knows freight eats margins. But few optimize it properly. By ensuring our trucks are always loaded 90–100%, we've saved huge costs. Drivers prefer full loads, and buyers appreciate that the freight per tonne comes down.

With optimized loads, clients don't push for unnecessary discounts because they see the efficiency.

Core Idea

Full trucks bring full trust.

Faster Money Rotation = Faster Decisions

Speed doesn't just apply to material; it applies to money as well. Faster money rotation means you can take bold decisions in raw material purchasing.

I recall a deal where I had to purchase raw materials in very large quantities. Many traders hesitated because their cash was stuck in slow cycles. But since our money rotated quickly, I could purchase instantly and secure the raw material at the right price.

Core Idea

In steel trading, raw material is the real asset.

If you can't move fast, you can't make a profit.

Cross-Selling Creates Flow

Another way to increase frequency is to widen what you sell. At a recent partners' meet, **I presented our full product range. Many long-time associates didn't even know we produced certain items!** Once they learned, they started ordering our ferro alloys and silico manganese too.

The result? More orders for us. More commissions for them.

In short, Cross-selling = growth for the company and the entire network.

Core Idea

In steel trading, raw material is the real asset.

If you can't move fast, you can't make a profit.

Human Touch Matters

No system can replace the power of personal visits. Whether it's suppliers, transporters, or buyers, nothing beats face-to-face trust.

Frequent visits keep relationships alive. A handshake, a conversation, a cup of tea together, these build bonds that last longer than any rate sheet.

In the end, we are humans dealing with humans.

Common Mistakes Traders Make With Frequency

Even when traders understand the importance of frequency, many unknowingly sabotage their own efforts through common operational mistakes. These errors are damaging because they create the opposite of what frequency is meant to achieve. Instead of building trust and reliability, they create frustration and unpredictability for customers.

Here are the five most frequent mistakes that prevent traders from achieving the consistency that frequency requires:

1. **Poor planning:** Leaving dispatches until the last minute always leads to delays and disappointed customers. This creates anxiety for buyers who can't plan their own operations around uncertain delivery times.
2. **Cash flow mismanagement:** Getting money stuck in credit-heavy deals with long payment schedules slows down the entire rotation cycle. When cash doesn't move, inventory can't move, and frequency becomes impossible.
3. **Over-dependence on 1–2 products:** Limited product variety restricts your order quantity. If you only sell TMT bars, customers might order once a month, but if you also offer pipes and strips, they might order weekly.
4. **Ignoring site coordination:** Imagine trucks arriving at construction sites, but they can't get unloaded because nobody coordinated with the site team in advance. This breaks the delivery rhythm and wastes everyone's time and money.

5. **Mistaking speed for shortcuts:** Rushing through processes without proper systems actually damages trust instead of building it. Customers value reliable speed, not unmanaged urgency that leads to errors and problems.

Implementation: How to Start Improving Frequency Today

Reading and understanding frequency is useful, but the real value comes from taking action.

The good news is that you don't need to overhaul your entire business overnight. Frequency can be improved through small, practical changes that build momentum over time. Most traders can see noticeable improvements within 90 days by focusing on the fundamentals.

Start with these six concrete steps that address the core elements of frequency in steel trading:

Step 1: Audit your dispatch system: Review how you currently handle orders. Do you plan loads in advance, or do you struggle each morning with them? An honest assessment of your current process is the starting point for improvement.

Step 2: Diversify your product range: Add 2–3 complementary products to your existing line so you can cross-sell to current customers. This creates more opportunities for frequent orders from the same buyers.

Step 3: Reduce minimum order quantities: Encourage smaller, more frequent orders instead of large, infrequent ones. This keeps money moving and customers engaged with your business regularly.

Step 4: Optimize truck utilization: Target 90–100% load capacity every time by combining different products and coordinating multiple deliveries. This reduces freight cost per tonne for everyone.

Step 5: Track and improve cash cycles: Measure how long it takes from order to payment, then work systematically to shorten this window by at least 20%. Faster money rotation enables everything else.

Step 6: Increase face-to-face contact: Double your physical visits with buyers and suppliers. Personal relationships still drive business decisions, especially in steel trading.

Why Frequency Matters More Today

The steel trading business has changed significantly in recent years, making frequency more important than ever.

In the past, buyers were comfortable waiting 7–10 days for material delivery. Today, they expect real-time tracking of deliveries, item dispatches within 48–72 hours, and timely updates about their orders.

In the past, relationships with traders were enough to keep customers loyal. Today, they need speed plus reliability to build longstanding trust. It means consistently delivering what you promise when you promise it. This combination has become the new foundation for customer loyalty.

This shift happened because technology made faster operations possible, and then customers began expecting them as standard. GPS tracking, CRM systems, WhatsApp updates, and ERP software have raised expectations across the entire industry, making frequency not just an advantage but a necessity for staying competitive.

The F.A.S.T. Framework in Action (F = Frequency)

When you get frequency right, it improves three important areas of your business:

1. **Material Flow:** Your dispatches become predictable, trucks run full, and deliveries happen smoothly without delays or problems.
2. **Funds Flow:** Orders happen more often in smaller amounts, less money gets stuck waiting, and cash moves faster through your business.
3. **Customer Flow:** You visit customers regularly and offer them multiple products, creating more opportunities for sales throughout the month.

Frequency is not about rushing around without thinking. It's about creating a steady, reliable pattern where your material, money, and customer relationships all move smoothly without constant problems and stress. This steady pattern is what changes trading from daily struggling into smooth and predictable business growth.

In Chapter 3, we saw how traders everywhere are tested by volatility, payment delays, and supply disruptions. These problems often look like external forces beyond our control.

In reality, many of them can be softened or even solved through frequency.

- **Market volatility:** When your money moves faster through smaller deals, you're not stuck holding expensive inventory when prices drop. You can buy and sell quickly, which protects you from sudden price changes.
- **Payment delays:** When you do many smaller transactions instead of a few large ones, one delayed payment won't hurt your entire cash flow. Money keeps moving even if one customer is slow to pay.
- **Supply chain disruptions:** When you have regular delivery schedules, full trucks, and good coordination with construction sites, your customers can keep working even when other suppliers face problems.

In other words, **frequency is stability disguised as speed.** It is what turns uncertainty into predictability and hesitation into trust.

That is why we start FAST with Frequency: it is the habit that gives traders control in a market that otherwise feels uncontrollable.

And once frequency is mastered, the next natural question is:

"How do I ensure every transaction is reliable?"

That brings us to the second pillar of the FAST framework: Availability. Because speed without availability doesn't build trust; it breaks it. And in steel trading, one wrong delivery can undo years of relationships.

CHAPTER 6

Availability: One-Stop Sourcing Advantage

In the last chapter, we discussed frequency and how faster cycles of buying and selling protect traders from volatility, speed up cash flow, and strengthen customer relationships. But frequency alone cannot work without its natural partner: **availability.**

You may plan the fastest dispatches and shortest rotations, but if the right material is not available when the customer requests it, your entire system collapses. That's why in the FAST framework, Availability is the "A", the backbone that keeps the engine running.

Why Availability is Non-Negotiable

A Real-World Experience

A builder called up their usual vendor on Monday morning and said, "Sir, I need 50 tonnes of 16mm TMT by Wednesday. My concreting is scheduled."

The vendor immediately promised delivery, but then realized that they didn't have stock.

The vendor and the builder both tried calling other suppliers to somehow get delivery on time, but it's too late. The earliest that the material can reach is Friday.

What just happened?

- That builder's 80 workers sat idle for two days.
- His project got delayed.
- The monsoon was approaching, so now the builder had to wait another month to resume work.
- He lost ₹3-4 lakhs in delays and escalations.
- His client lost trust in him, and he lost trust in the vendor.
- The builder will definitely not go back to that vendor.

When material is not available as promised, the costs multiply fast:

1. **Idle labour costs:** 50–100 workers waiting at a construction site can cost lakhs in wasted wages, even when they're not working productively.

2. **Rising project costs:** Delayed supplies during monsoons can stall entire construction sites, leading to cost escalations of ₹2–5 lakh per week as everything else gets pushed back.
3. **Lost credibility:** A promoter under pressure blames the contractor, and the contractor blames the supplier. Ultimately, it's the trader's reputation that gets damaged in the market.

A builder may forget a rate difference of ₹200 per tonne within a few months. But he will never forget the day his project stalled because the steel didn't arrive when promised. This is why availability becomes more important than small price differences.

Single-Point Sourcing = Customer Simplicity

Modern construction projects require multiple types of steel products, and managing relationships with several different suppliers creates complexity and delays. We recognized this challenge and designed our operations to solve it.

Our single-point sourcing approach means buyers can lift everything they need from one location, like pipes, TMT, strips, or Silico manganese 60-14.

For contractors, this simplified approach delivers several practical benefits:

1. No running between different factories saves time and transportation costs
2. Lower overall transport costs through consolidated deliveries
3. Faster negotiations with one trusted supplier instead of multiple vendors

4. One-stop accountability when problems arise or changes are needed

The principle is simple: the more problems we solve for customers, the less they need to look elsewhere for solutions.

Flexibility Without Overstocking

Availability comes with an inherent risk that many traders struggle to manage effectively. Holding too much inventory blocks cash flow and erodes profit margins through carrying costs and potential obsolescence.

We've learned to balance availability with financial discipline through these practical approaches:

- **Buyer discipline:** We work with customers who lift materials promptly and filter out those who create excessive delays in pickup.
- **Smart volume planning:** Stock variety is maintained, but in carefully calculated volumes based on actual demand patterns rather than guesswork.
- **Built-in rotation:** We plan stock movements so that inventory keeps flowing and nothing sits idle for extended periods gathering dust.

This balanced approach allows us to stay available for customers without turning our warehouses into dead capital that hurts cash flow and profitability.

The 60–70% Stock Rule

Managing inventory requires a disciplined approach that balances customer service with cash flow management. At BS Group, we've developed what we call the golden rule of stock management.

We maintain 60–70% of SKUs in ready stock at all times. Whether customers need straight bars, bends, or specific sizes, like 8mm, 10mm, 12mm, 16mm, 20mm, 25mm, or 32mm, our buyers know they'll find what they need when they visit us.

This rule works because it covers the most common requirements without tying up excessive capital in slow-moving inventory. We treat this stock not as a cost burden, but as a loyalty investment that keeps customers coming back.

How Availability Translates to Growth

Most traders think availability is just about having stock ready, so they don't disappoint customers. But it's how you build a business that grows faster than competitors who only compete on price.

Think about it this way: when customers know you always have what they need, something interesting happens. They stop shopping around. They stop calling three other suppliers for quotes. They just call you directly because they trust you'll deliver.

When you consistently maintain availability, several positive changes happen:

1. Higher customer retention rates develop because buyers who never hear "not available" naturally become more loyal to your business.
2. Premium pricing becomes possible as contractors willingly pay slightly more for the certainty and peace of mind that comes with a reliable supply.
3. Reduced sales effort is required because when buyers trust you have stock ready, they stop shopping around with competitors for every order.
4. Sustainable competitive advantage emerges because while others compete purely on price, you win on reliability and peace of mind.

Common Mistakes Traders Make

Most traders fail at availability, not because they don't understand its importance, but because they make predictable planning and execution errors that undermine their efforts.

These mistakes happen frequently across the industry:

- **Poor stock planning:** Keeping large quantities of one product while running completely out of others that customers actually need more frequently.
- **Over-reliance on single suppliers:** When that one key supplier faces delays or problems, the entire supply chain breaks down, and customers suffer.
- **Cash mismanagement:** Tying up working capital in slow-moving stock while leaving no liquidity available for faster-selling items that customers want immediately.

Implementation Steps: How to Improve Availability

Improving availability requires systematic planning and disciplined execution rather than random inventory buying. These steps provide a practical roadmap for any trader looking to strengthen their availability without destroying cash flow.

Start with these fundamental improvements:

Step 1: Study demand patterns: Analyze which sizes and grades move fastest in your specific market area, then prioritize keeping those items in stock consistently.

Step 2: Maintain strategic buffers: Even during low season, keep at least 30% of key SKUs ready so you can respond immediately when demand picks up.

Step 3: Develop single-point sourcing: Build relationships with suppliers who can provide multiple products efficiently, reducing your complexity and customer wait times.

Step 4: Discipline customer behavior: Work with buyers who lift materials promptly and avoid long delays that tie up your working capital unnecessarily.

Step 5: Review and adjust monthly: Regularly evaluate which SKUs are becoming dead stock and adjust your purchasing strategy accordingly to maintain optimal inventory health.

Managing Space Constraints

Many traders worry about having enough physical space for maintaining proper inventory levels. This concern is valid but manageable with the right approach.

Start with high-rotation SKUs even if space is limited. Maintaining just 3–4 key sizes in smaller quantities still builds customer confidence and demonstrates reliability. Partner with suppliers who can provide quick replenishments when you need to restock popular items.

The key is starting where you are, rather than waiting until you have perfect facilities. Consistent small-scale availability beats inconsistent large-scale inventory.

Calculating Optimal Stock Levels

- **Determining the right inventory levels** requires understanding your actual sales patterns rather than guessing based on general market trends or supplier recommendations.
- **Track your average monthly sales for each SKU** over at least three months to establish baseline demand. Keep 30–40% buffer stock for your top 5 fastest-moving SKUs to ensure you never run out during peak demand periods.
- **For slower-moving items, maintain minimum quantities** sufficient to avoid disappointing customers while not tying up excessive working capital in inventory that moves infrequently.

Managing Cash Flow with Higher Inventory

Maintaining availability does require more working capital, but this challenge can be managed through operational improvements that maintain liquidity.

Work with suppliers who offer smaller minimum order quantities, which allows more frequent restocking without large capital commitments. Increase the frequency of inventory rotations as discussed in Chapter 5 to keep cash moving through faster cycles.

Most importantly, avoid working with buyers who consistently delay material pickup. Cash flow health depends on inventory movement, not inventory accumulation.

The “A” in FAST

Availability serves as the foundation that makes frequency possible and profitable. At BS Group, our availability strategy creates a complete system that supports all other business objectives.

Our approach includes maintaining 60–70% of SKUs ready at all times, providing sourcing simplicity through multiple products under one roof, balancing variety with smart cash flow management, and delivering peace of mind so buyers stop shopping around.

In steel trading, availability equals customer loyalty. The builder who knows that BS always has material ready doesn’t waste time checking with competitors for every requirement.

When you successfully combine frequency (fast cycles) with availability (one-stop readiness), you survive market challenges and create a competitive moat that other traders cannot easily copy or replicate.

In the next chapter, we'll move to the "S" of FAST: **Savings.** Because once you've built frequency and availability, the real edge comes from cutting costs smartly, so every transaction becomes more profitable than the last.

CHAPTER 7

Savings: Profit Hidden in Costs

If Frequency accelerates your cash flow and Availability wins loyalty, then Savings is what secures your margins.

Too many traders think growth comes only from selling more steel. But profits don't just come from higher sales; they go out through poor cost management. Every half-empty truck you send, every rusted tonne getting wasted, every delayed dispatch quietly reduces your margins while you're busy chasing the next order.

Savings doesn't mean taking shortcuts. It means creating a disciplined system where no rupee, truck, or tonne goes to waste. This pillar ensures that your growth is not just bigger in volume, but stronger in profitability.

Where Most Traders Lose Money

Most traders can tell you their selling prices down to the last rupee, but if you ask them about their hidden costs, they get vague. This gap between what they know and what they don't know is where profits disappear.

The traders unknowingly reduce their profit margins in three predictable places:

Freight costs: Sending half-filled trucks means paying double for the same journey. If you're moving 25 tonnes in a truck that can carry 50 tonnes, you're essentially paying twice the freight cost per tonne.

Material wastage: Rusted pipes, broken TMT bars, and mishandled loading and unloading turn sellable inventory into expensive scrap that hurts your bottom line.

Poor market timing: Buying stock when prices are high and being forced to sell at a loss when rates fall because you didn't plan your inventory cycles properly.

Most traders focus obsessively on "selling price" while completely ignoring these silent killers. But the truth is that sales can increase your revenue, while savings protect your survival.

Traditional vs. FAST Process

Let me show you exactly how the right system saves money through a real example. Imagine you have a customer who needs both TMT bars and pipes for their project.

The traditional way most traders handle this:

They'd source TMT from one factory and pipes from another because that's how their supplier relationships work. Now they're dealing with two locations, which creates coordination headaches and costs them 4 days just managing logistics.

They need two separate trucks, tying up ₹30 lakh in working capital. They need 4 laborers, but half their time gets wasted on coordination issues. By the time everything reaches the customer, 8 days have passed.

Better integrated approach:

Source both TMT and pipes from a single campus, so the entire order gets fulfilled in just 1 day. Use one optimized truck, spend only ₹10k total, and you need just 2 laborers working efficiently.

The result is lower costs, faster dispatch, and happier customers who get their complete order in one day instead of eight.

Implementation Roadmap

Saving money systematically requires a structured approach rather than random cost-cutting efforts. Most traders try to save money by haggling over small expenses while missing the big leaks that really hurt profitability.

Here's how to implement savings systematically:

First, identify where money is leaking:

- Audit your last 3 months of freight bills. How many trucks went out half-empty?
- Check your storage areas for rusted or damaged stock. What percentage of inventory became unsellable?
- Compare your buying rates versus selling rates during market volatility periods to see where timing hurts you.

Next, track and measure consistently:

- Use a simple Excel sheet or CRM system to log wastage, idle vehicle days, and freight costs per truck.

- Review your monthly savings percentage compared to your total sales to understand trends.

Then prioritize the biggest problems:

- Fix the largest leaks first, which are usually freight optimization and material wastage.
- After those are under control, tackle sourcing costs and customer delays that tie up working capital.

Finally, implement systematic controls:

- Plan mixed loads that combine pipes, TMT, and strips in single shipments.
- Invest in covered storage facilities to reduce rust and weather damage.
- Set clear policies for buyers: delayed material lifting means no future credit deals.

Measurement & Tracking

To make savings a reliable system rather than occasional luck, you need to track cost management like you track sales performance.

Monitor these key performance indicators regularly:

- Freight cost per tonne moved
- Percentage of inventory lost to wastage each quarter
- Number of idle truck days that generate cost without revenue
- Average number of days inventory sits before sale
- Net margin retained after all operational costs

Review your performance monthly for cost overruns, quarterly for supplier efficiency and freight contracts, and annually to benchmark your savings percentage against industry standards.

5 Cost-Saving Habits Every Trader Should Practice

Building a culture of intelligent savings requires developing daily habits that become automatic rather than requiring constant decision-making.

Make these five practices part of your regular operations:

- **Optimize every truck load:** Never send vehicles out half-filled when you could combine orders or add complementary products to maximize capacity.
- **Prevent wastage before it starts:** Cover inventory properly, train loading crews to handle materials carefully, and inspect storage areas regularly.
- **Trust the source, not just the price:** Pay slightly more for reliable suppliers to avoid the hidden costs of quality problems and delays.
- **Find value in byproducts:** Look for ways to reuse or sell what you currently consider waste; there's often unexpected profit hiding there.
- **Maintain zero-delay policies:** Keep inventory rotating and cash flowing by avoiding situations where materials or money sit idle.

Advanced Savings Strategies

Once you've mastered the basics of cost control, there are more sophisticated strategies that can significantly improve your profitability over time. These strategies require longer-term thinking but create sustainable competitive advantages:

- **Bulk purchasing agreements:** Negotiate long-term contracts with suppliers during low-demand seasons when you have more leverage and they need consistent orders.
- **Seasonal buying patterns:** Purchase raw materials when market prices dip predictably, such as before monsoon seasons when demand typically softens.
- **Transportation partnerships:** Work with truckers for fixed monthly rates instead of per-trip pricing, which gives you cost predictability and often lower overall rates.
- **Insurance and risk management:** Protect against theft, delays, or catastrophic losses to avoid situations that can wipe out months of profit in a single incident.

Common Mistakes Traders Make

Even when traders understand the importance of saving money, they often make predictable mistakes that backfire and cost more than they save. These mistakes happen because traders focus on the wrong things:

- **Over-cutting costs:** Sacrificing quality or customer service in the name of savings. This always backfires by losing customers who are worth much more than the money saved.

- **Overstocking inventory:** Thinking "more stock equals more ready sales," but ending up with blocked capital and storage costs that eat into profits.
- **Short-term thinking:** Saving ₹100 today by choosing the cheapest supplier, but losing ₹10 lakh tomorrow when that supplier delivers poor quality or delays shipments.
- **No measurement system:** Traders who don't track costs systematically often don't realize where their margins are disappearing until it's too late.

The Real Power of Savings

Savings aren't about becoming cheap or pinching every penny. They're about creating operational discipline that frees up capacity and resources for growth opportunities. When your costs are properly controlled, 20–30% of your capital and time get freed up from wasteful activities. That freed capacity can fuel new orders, entry into new markets, and service to more customers.

The formula is simple:

Better Savings leads to Higher Margins, which creates More Freedom, which enables More Growth.

Savings as a Growth Multiplier

In the F.A.S.T. Framework, Savings is the silent multiplier. While Frequency fuels momentum and Availability builds loyalty, Savings ensures every tonne sold contributes maximum margin. And here's the real beauty: Savings makes you competitive without cutting rates. With leaner costs, you can price better, serve better, and still retain profits.

In the next chapter, we move to the final pillar: Time: the real currency of steel trading. Because when you save money, you gain margin. But when you save time, you gain growth.

CHAPTER 8

Time: The Real Currency

In steel trading, margins are measured in rupees, but growth is measured in minutes. If money is the fuel of business, time is its real currency.

The "T" in the F.A.S.T. Growth Framework represents Time.

Not just clock hours, but the efficiency with which you plan, execute, and deliver.

Time is what keeps furnaces running, projects moving, and trust alive. When you save time, you don't just save cost, you build reliability. And reliability is what keeps customers coming back.

Timing is Everything

Every experienced trader will tell you the same thing: timing can make or break your entire business. You don't just have to be fast, but smart with when you buy, when you sell, and when you deliver.

The harsh reality is that poor timing kills profits faster than any other mistake:

1. Buy in the wrong market cycle, and losses multiply quickly as prices fall after your purchase.
2. Sell too late in a rising market, and your margins evaporate as competitors grab the best rates.

3. Deliver late to construction sites, and you lose customers who can't afford project delays.

Timing isn't Just Luck: A Real Story

Timing isn't guesswork or luck. It comes from staying connected by daily conversations with suppliers, stockists, customers, and fellow traders.

It gives you the market pulse that others miss.

A trader who talks to 10 different people every day knows what's happening in the market far better than someone who just waits for official updates or relies on yesterday's information.

The more actively you stay connected, the sharper your timing becomes.

Let me share a story that changed how I think about time in this business.

Once, we were supplying steel to the Sarda Energy Hydro Project, a major infrastructure development project.

For this client, even a single day's delay meant cost escalations running into lakhs and immense pressure on contractors who had committed to strict project timelines.

We made sure every dispatch reached exactly when needed. Not once did they have to chase us or worry about their schedule.

The Results:

- Repeat orders.
- Long-term loyalty.
- And a reputation for reliability that helped us win more projects across the region.

The Lesson:

Timely delivery is a brand-builder that pays dividends for years.

How Time Creates Savings

Most traders don't realize how closely time and money are connected in daily operations.

Every minute you save in one area creates cost savings in multiple other areas.

Consider these:

1. **Faster dispatches reduce demurrage charges** and labor costs from workers waiting around for delayed trucks.
2. **Quicker cash rotation means less working capital sits idle** in the pipeline, freeing up money for better purchasing opportunities.
3. **On-time deliveries eliminate penalties,** disputes, and the hidden costs of rebuilding damaged relationships.

Every hour saved through better systems becomes invisible profit that flows directly to your bottom line without any additional sales effort.

Common Issues & Mistakes in Time Management

Even traders who understand the importance of time often lose hours and days through predictable operational mistakes that can be easily avoided with better planning.

Here's where most time gets wasted:

1. **Paper-based processes** that require physical signatures, manual invoices, and in-person approvals slow everything down in our digital age.
2. **Half-filled trucks** happen when traders wait days trying to fill complete loads instead of planning mixed-material dispatches that optimize capacity immediately.
3. **Poor communication** leaves buyers, suppliers, and transporters without real-time updates, leading to confusion and delays.
4. **Unclear accountability** means no one takes ownership of moving bottlenecks along, so problems just sit until they become emergencies.
5. **Rushing quality checks** might seem like a time-saver, but it causes rejections and returns that double the time lost.

To identify your biggest time drains, track how long dispatch approvals take, where trucks spend idle time, and how often delayed payments hold up dispatch readiness. Fix these systematic issues, and you'll free up hours every week.

Daily Time Management Habits for Traders

Building excellence in time management requires developing daily habits that become automatic rather than requiring constant decision-making.

Make these practices part of your regular routine:

1. Plan every dispatch systematically instead of leaving logistics to chance or last-minute scrambling.
2. Assign dedicated resources to bottlenecks so that known problem areas always have someone focused on keeping them moving.
3. Align financial readiness with supply commitments to ensure payment capability matches your delivery promises.
4. Stay connected daily with market contacts because timing improves with constant exposure to real market conditions.

Time Management Tools & Systems

The right technology doesn't replace human relationships; it amplifies them with speed and reliability that manual processes can't match. (We will talk about the tools more deeply in Chapter 10.)

These tools make time management scalable as your business grows:

GPS and IoT tracking show truck locations in real time, allowing proactive problem-solving before delays impact customers.

ERP and CRM integration connects dispatch, approvals, and billing in one system instead of requiring separate manual coordination.

Automated notifications give buyers proactive updates, reducing the time spent on status calls and relationship management.

Cloud-based records provide instant access to invoices, test certificates, and weighbridge reports from anywhere, eliminating delays caused by missing paperwork.

When implemented thoughtfully, technology amplifies human trust with speed and accuracy that creates competitive advantages.

A few years ago, I remember doing everything the old way, calling people constantly, chasing approvals, playing phone tag all day long. It was exhausting, and we were always behind schedule.

Then we realized that while we were busy making phone calls, our competitors were using systems that did the work automatically. We were losing business because we were slower to respond and update customers.

That's when we decided to embrace the tools that could actually help us serve customers better. At BS group, we've integrated all these systems so that time never slips through organizational cracks or communication gaps.

Transforming Dispatch Planning

Dispatch planning can be a daily headache. Paperwork moves slowly across different departments, and hours get wasted getting approvals from various people who aren't available when needed.

If this is one problem you are going through, then you need to transform this process through systematic changes:

- **Dedicated resources at bottlenecks:** Identify where delays always happen and put specific people in charge of keeping those areas moving smoothly.
- **Real-time tracking systems:** GPS and digital dashboards let you see exactly where every truck and order stood at any moment.
- **Integrated digital workflows:** Approvals, documentation, and communication should all happen through connected systems instead of separate manual processes.

We have already implemented all this at the BS Group, and now, one short phone call is enough to trigger our entire dispatch chain. Trucks, paperwork, and payments all move together in coordination instead of creating delays for each other.

Aligning Financial Readiness with Supply Flow

Time management in steel trading isn't just about physical logistics; it's also about financial timing. Suppliers consistently prefer working with buyers who pay on time, even over those who might offer slightly better rates but have unpredictable payment patterns.

Learn to align your financial flow with your supply flow, ensuring payments are never delayed, and suppliers prioritize your orders.

When cash flow stays steady and predictable, supply flow becomes fast and reliable. And when supply flow operates smoothly, business growth compounds naturally.

This financial discipline creates a positive cycle: reliable payments earn supplier trust, which gets you priority service, which helps you serve customers better, which generates more revenue to maintain reliable payments.

The "T" in Action: BS Benchmarks

Make time management your competitive edge through consistent daily practices that compound over months and years.

We did the same a few years back, and our current benchmarks demonstrate what's possible with systematic time management:

90% of planned deliveries execute without delays, giving customers predictable project timelines they can count on.

30% time savings in loading and unloading through process optimization that benefits both our efficiency and customer operations.

50% faster repeat orders through systematic mapping and preparation that turns returning customers into quick, profitable transactions.

40% less working capital tied up due to aligned financial and supply flows that keep money moving productively.

While other companies might achieve 20–30% efficiency in these areas, we maintain 80–90% performance daily. This consistency is why developers see us as partners who respect their time and project requirements.

The Complete FAST Framework Advantage

With Time, the F.A.S.T. Framework creates a complete system that transforms steel trading from reactive survival into proactive growth:

Frequency makes money rotate faster through shorter, more efficient cycles.

Availability ensures customers stay loyal because they can count on you to have what they need.

Savings protect margins and free up capital for growth opportunities instead of waste.

Time multiplies trust, speed, and growth by making everything else work more efficiently.

Together, these four pillars transform steel trading from a daily survival game into a predictable, system-driven growth engine that compounds results over time.

Implementation Timeline for FAST

Most traders can start seeing visible improvements within 3–6 months of systematic implementation. The key is building one pillar at a time instead of trying to change everything simultaneously.

Start with Frequency through better dispatch planning, then add Availability through disciplined stock management. Integrate Savings through systematic cost controls, and finally refine Time through system-wide efficiency improvements.

Here are some common mistakes you can avoid while implementing the FAST Framework-

1. **Don't implement FAST halfway** by picking one pillar and ignoring the others; they work together as a complete system.
2. **Avoid cutting corners** in the name of short-term savings or speed, which undermines the long-term trust and reliability that makes the system powerful.
3. **Always measure progress with proper tracking and KPIs,** because what gets measured gets improved consistently.

In the end, the traders who succeed long-term are not those who move the most tonnes, but those who move them frequently, reliably, profitably, and on time. That consistent excellence is the true power of being F.A.S.T.

CHAPTER 9

The B.S. Process: Trust Built Over Decades

In the last four chapters, we explored the FAST Framework: Frequency, Availability, Savings, and Time, as the foundation of system-driven trading. But here's what we learned:

Frameworks only work when you actually live them every day.

At BS Group, we realized early that having a great strategy on paper means nothing if you can't execute it consistently. Traders needed more than just speed, stock, savings, and timing; they needed a trust-based process that would hold everything together when challenges arose.

That's how the B.S. Process was born: a system where trust isn't just a feeling or promise, but an actual process with clear steps and accountability.

What is the B.S. Process?

The BS Process is our way of building trust into every single transaction through systems, transparency, and accountability. It's not about being the cheapest supplier or making the loudest marketing claims in the market.

Instead, it's about becoming the most reliable partner, where dealers know that problems will be solved quickly, promises will be honored completely, and their business growth will never be compromised by our unreliability.

The Four Core Pillars of the BS Process

Trust doesn't happen by accident or through good intentions alone. It requires specific, repeatable actions that dealers can count on in every interaction. Our process is built on four pillars that address the most common pain points dealers face when working with steel suppliers.

1. Dealer-Friendly Systems

Most steel suppliers treat dealer problems as interruptions to their business. We treat them as opportunities to build stronger relationships. When dealers face issues, they need solutions, not excuses or blame-shifting.

Here's how our dealer-friendly approach works in practice:

1. Dedicated support for dispatch coordination and paperwork handling, so dealers don't waste time chasing multiple people for simple tasks.
2. Fast escalation systems that move problems up the chain immediately instead of letting them sit unresolved for days.
3. Proactive updates that reach dealers before they even need to ask about order status or delivery timing.

The result is that dealers feel heard, valued, and supported, which naturally leads to higher loyalty and more repeat business.

Let me share a real scenario. While working with us, a dealer once faced repeated confusion about TMT bar sizes in his orders. So, instead of passing the blame to our production team or asking him to call different departments, our team gave him instant clarity and dispatched mixed loads within hours. He told us later, "I call BS first because I know you won't give me tension."

2. 100% Transparency in Dealings

In steel trading, price volatility creates constant uncertainty for dealers. They never know if the rate they get today will be the same rate their competitor gets tomorrow, or if sudden price changes will make their committed orders unprofitable.

We eliminate this uncertainty through complete transparency:

1. Daily price guidelines are shared openly with all dealers, so everyone knows they're getting fair treatment.
2. No rate changes after commitment, even if market prices spike unexpectedly, and we could make more money by breaking our word.
3. Lab-tested BIS quality backing every deal, with test certificates provided for complete transparency.

This approach gives dealers predictability and peace of mind that they can plan their business around.

Here's a perfect example of how this works. When market prices shot up by 8% in a single week, we still honored the lower committed rates for all buyers who had placed orders that day.

It was a short-term financial loss for us, but it created long-term loyalty worth crores.

3. Zero-Gap Responsibility

The steel industry is full of finger-pointing when problems occur. Suppliers blame transporters, transporters blame sites, and dealers get caught in the middle trying to resolve issues that aren't technically their fault.

We take a completely different approach: if a problem affects our dealer, we own it and solve it immediately, regardless of where the technical liability lies.

Our zero-gap responsibility means:

1. Immediate resolution even when the liability technically belongs to someone else in the supply chain.
2. Insurance and cost recovery are handled separately later; dealer confidence comes first, and paperwork comes second.

This approach builds unshakeable trust because dealers know BS will stand by its word in every situation, not just the easy ones.

4. Real-Time Tracking & Support

Trust requires visibility. Dealers need to know where their orders stand without having to make phone calls or send WhatsApp messages chasing updates.

We make trust visible through technology:

1. GPS-enabled trucks tracked by our CRM team provide real-time location data for every shipment.
2. Automated buyer updates send messages like "Truck has left," "2 days away," and "Delivered" without dealers having to ask.

3. Lab testing results are shared digitally for complete transparency about quality standards.

The result is zero anxiety for dealers. They don't need to ask "Mera maal kahan hai?", they already know exactly where it is and when it will arrive.

After implementing GPS tracking and automated CRM updates, we cut dealer complaint calls by 70%. That time saved gets reinvested in selling more and building stronger relationships.

If I had to capture our entire approach in one simple line, it would be this: "Quality speaks. Trust delivers."

This promise translates into specific, measurable commitments:

1. 100% break-free, low-carbon steel that meets or exceeds industry standards.
2. Lab-tested BIS quality with certificates provided.
3. Zero variation in sizes and thickness.
4. Personalized service by BS experts who understand each dealer's specific needs.
5. After-sales support, including daily price updates, technical guidance, and faster issue resolution.

For dealers, these commitments solve their biggest daily headaches:

1. Fewer disputes over quality or specifications
2. More opportunities for cross-selling because they trust our complete product range
3. Faster repeat orders and customer referrals because reliability builds its own reputation.

Why the BS Process Matters

Dealers today face a fundamental choice that determines their long-term success or failure.

They can either follow the traditional market cycle: fighting margin wars, chasing discounts, and losing peace of mind, or they can build their business on trust-driven systems that solve problems, protect margins, and create sustainable growth.

At BS Group, we chose the second path early in our journey. That's why our growth has not only been faster, but also more sustainable than competitors who rely purely on price competition.

Financial Impact: The ROI of Trust

The numbers tell the story clearly. Before implementing our trust-based process, we dealt with frequent disputes, slow dispatch times, and hidden costs that eroded margins. We spent too much time fighting for each deal and not enough time building lasting relationships.

After implementing the BS Process, everything changed:

- Higher customer retention because dealers stopped shopping around for every order
- Premium pricing ability because dealers willingly pay more for reliability
- Reduced sales effort because trust pulls in repeat orders automatically
- Stronger referrals that create higher lifetime dealer value.

I've seen dealers who started with small orders grow their business with us significantly over time. This growth happened because of reliability and support, not because we offered the cheapest rates. In short, trust builds business relationships that price competition simply can't match.

Implementation Guide: Building Your Own Trust-Based Process

You don't need to be BS Group's size to implement trust-based systems. Any trader can start building these practices and see results within months.

Start with these fundamental steps:

- **Step 1: Fix your biggest system gaps-** Identify the three biggest pain points your dealers face: usually dispatch delays, paperwork confusion, and payment issues, then build simple systems to address these consistently.
- **Step 2: Practice complete transparency-** Share daily rates openly, maintain consistent quality standards, and never go

back on commitments even when market changes make it financially tempting.

- **Step 3: Own problems immediately-** When issues occur, solve them first and worry about recovering costs later. This single practice can lock in dealer loyalty for years.
- **Step 4: Use technology to make trust visible-** GPS tracking, CRM systems, digital invoicing, and electronic weighbridge records don't replace trust, but they make it visible and measurable.
- **Step 5: Build relationships, not just transactions-** Focus on long-term partnerships rather than one-time deals. A single loyal dealer is worth more than chasing ten occasional buyers.

Common Questions About Trust-Based Trading

When I share the BS Process with other traders, they often have practical questions about how this actually works in real business situations. These are smart, legitimate concerns that deserve honest answers.

Let me walk through the questions that come up most frequently:

"Trust doesn't pay the bills."

Actually, it does, and often better than price competition. When dealers trust you completely, they reorder faster, lift larger volumes, and refer other customers. That loyalty compounds into steady revenue that's much more valuable than occasional big deals.

"This approach sounds expensive."

Trust-based systems do require upfront investment, but compare that cost to losing one major dealer, dealing with one payment default, or having one large order cancelled. Trust pays back many times over through reduced customer acquisition costs and higher lifetime value.

"I don't have the scale that BS has."

You don't need a large scale to build trust. Start with one improved system, one transparent practice, or one act of taking responsibility. Trust grows deal by deal, not through grand gestures.

Why Every Trader Needs a BS Process

The BS Process isn't just for BS Group; it's a blueprint that any trader can adapt to their own market and circumstances. The specific systems might be different, but the principle remains the same.

Because systems + sincerity = trust.

And trust = long-term growth.

In the end, your real product isn't just steel, it's certainty.

You're selling peace of mind, reliability, and the confidence that comes from working with someone who keeps their word.

When you make certainty your brand, dealers stop comparing your rates to competitors and start comparing relationships instead. That's when your business stops being just another trading firm and starts becoming irreplaceable in your market.

This transformation doesn't happen overnight, but it starts with the very next transaction you handle. Each time you choose transparency over secrecy, responsibility over blame-shifting, and systems over chaos, you build trust that compounds over the years into an advantage that no price-cutting competitor can easily replicate.

CHAPTER 10

Digital in Steel Trading

In the last section, we explored the FAST Framework and the BS Process as the pillars of sustainable steel trading. But here's something I learned the hard way:

None of these systems can be executed consistently without digital tools backing them up.

Think about what actually happens when you try to implement FAST manually.

Frequency needs quick dispatch updates, mixed-load planning, and real-time follow-ups, all of which become chaos without proper systems.

Availability requires instant stock checks and visibility across multiple products, which is impossible to track on paper.

Savings depend on monitoring wastage, freight costs, and sourcing transparency, which requires data that manual processes can't capture accurately.

And **Time** gets wasted without digital approvals, automated alerts, and instant communication.

Digital tools work like the invisible engine behind FAST.

Without them, you might understand the theory perfectly, but execution collapses into delays, disputes, and lost trust. With them, trust and transparency multiply naturally.

The Rise of Digital Payments

Just a few years ago, steel trading still relied heavily on handwritten ledgers, cash transactions, and delayed bank drafts. I remember spending entire days just managing payment paperwork and waiting for cheques to clear.

Today, everything has changed through UPI, RTGS, NEFT, and modern digital banking systems. This transformation affects every aspect of how business gets done:

Instant transfers build immediate confidence between traders and suppliers because money moves as fast as promises.

Clean digital records reduce disputes significantly because every transaction has a clear trail that both parties can verify.

Faster payment cycles mean cash rotates quickly through your business, enabling reinvestment opportunities at exactly the right market timing.

I've watched deals close in minutes that once took days to complete, not because trucks started moving faster, but because money started moving instantly.

Without digital payments, liquidity gets stuck in the system, and disputes multiply. With digital payments, trust becomes visible and growth accelerates naturally.

WhatsApp Groups: The New Trading Floor

The traditional "adda", where traders used to gather at tea stalls, has completely shifted to WhatsApp groups. Daily rate updates, availability announcements, and even freight-sharing coordination now happen in real time through these digital spaces.

But there's a big difference between traders who add value and those who just add noise.

- You need to share clear rate information, update stock availability regularly, and respond quickly when someone asks a question. Over time, you will become the go-to person that everyone trusts for reliable information.
- On the other hand, some traders just forward random messages without any context or keep sharing outdated information. They might be active in the groups, but nobody really pays attention to what they say anymore.
- For us, WhatsApp isn't a distraction or time-waster; it's become a powerful relationship accelerator that keeps us connected to market pulse throughout the day.

CRM Tools: Discipline Behind the Scenes

Every trader has a sharp memory for important deals and relationships, but human memory isn't perfect, especially when managing hundreds of customers and thousands of transactions.

That's exactly why Customer Relationship Management systems have become essential rather than optional:

1. Follow-ups never get lost in the daily chaos because the system reminds you automatically when action is needed.
2. Payment reminders happen on schedule without you having to remember dates or track individual customer payment patterns.
3. Complete customer histories stay accessible instantly, so you can reference past deals, preferences, and issues during every conversation.

At BS Group, when we started using CRM properly and when we separated "relationship work" from "follow-up work," our productivity multiplied significantly. The CRM didn't replace personal trust and connection; it protected and strengthened those relationships by ensuring nothing important fell through the cracks.

Online Catalogs: Transparency Made Visible

Modern buyers don't want to keep calling suppliers to ask "Kya stock hai (What stock is available)?" every time they need something. They want instant visibility into what's available so they can plan their own operations efficiently.

Online catalogs and real-time stock lists solve this problem by allowing buyers to check availability instantly without bothering anyone. The market message is becoming very clear: when you embrace transparency, you consistently win more business, while traders who hide information or make access difficult lose customers to more open competitors.

Going Digital Step by Step

For traders who've built their business on traditional methods, the shift to digital tools can feel overwhelming. But it doesn't have to be complicated if you approach it systematically.

Here's how to make the transition manageable and profitable:

- **Step 1: Start with the basics-** Shift your payments to UPI and RTGS for instant transactions. Create a simple WhatsApp broadcast list for sharing daily rates with your regular customers.
- **Step 2: Add systematic discipline-** Implement a basic CRM system like Zoho, HubSpot, or even a well-organized Excel sheet with automated reminders. Start sharing clear availability updates daily so customers know what to expect.
- **Step 3: Embrace transparency-** Maintain a digital product catalog using Google Sheets or a simple website. Share test reports, invoices, and dispatch updates digitally so customers can track everything.
- **Step 4: Scale up systematically-** Add GPS tracking for your truck fleet. Integrate ERP systems with CRM for seamless operations. Automate alerts for dispatch notifications, payment reminders, and reorder suggestions.

The investment doesn't have to be massive. A basic setup with CRM, simple catalog, and WhatsApp costs ₹5–₹10k per month.

Advanced setups with full ERP, GPS integration, and automation run ₹50k+ monthly, but you can build toward that gradually.

Common Mistakes in Digital Transition

Digital transformation sounds straightforward in theory: just buy some software, train your team, and start operating more efficiently. But in reality, many traders rush into digital tools without proper planning and end up worse off than when they started. The technology works fine, but the implementation creates new problems that didn't exist before.

Even when traders understand the value of going digital, they often make predictable mistakes that waste money and create frustration instead of solving problems. Watch out for these common errors:

- **Overcomplicating too early** by buying a full ERP system when you've never properly used even basic Excel spreadsheets for business tracking.
- **Not training your team properly,** so digital tools fail because only the owner knows how to use them, while the staff continues old manual methods.
- **Poor integration planning** results in using five different apps with no connection between them, creating more chaos than the old manual system.
- **Ignoring company culture** by treating digital tools as a replacement for human trust rather than understanding that they must amplify existing relationships.

The key is remembering that technology should make your life easier, not more complicated. If your digital tools are creating more problems than they solve, you're probably moving too fast or choosing the wrong solutions for your current needs.

Start simple, master each tool completely, and then gradually add complexity as your team becomes comfortable with the new systems.

Answering The 'What Ifs' I Hear All the Time

When I talk to other traders about going digital, they often raise practical concerns that deserve honest answers:

"What if my suppliers or customers aren't ready for digital?"

Start with a hybrid approach. Accept cash and cheques, but maintain digital records yourself. Gradually encourage partners by showing how digital processes reduce disputes and save everyone time.

"What if the internet isn't reliable in remote areas?"

Use tools with offline sync capabilities like Google Sheets offline mode or mobile-based CRMs that upload updates automatically when connectivity returns.

"What if different tools don't work together?"

Choose platforms with API integrations from the beginning. Even basic CRMs today integrate smoothly with WhatsApp, banking systems, and invoicing software.

Digital + FAST + BS Process = Complete Growth System

Digital tools aren't separate from the FAST Framework and BS Process; they're the connecting tissue that makes everything work together seamlessly.

For the FAST Framework, digital systems ensure faster dispatches through automated planning, instant stock checks for availability, precise savings tracking through data analysis, and efficient time management through automation.

For the BS Process, digital tools make trust visible through GPS tracking, automated customer updates, transparent record-keeping, and CRM-driven communication that never drops important details.

Without digital support, FAST remains a good theory that's hard to execute consistently. With proper digital integration, FAST becomes a reliable execution that compounds results over time.

The Choice Every Trader Faces

Steel Trading 4.0 isn't coming someday; it's already here. The market has become transparent, buyers expect digital convenience, and successful competitors are adapting quickly to these new realities.

You have a clear choice to make. If you resist digital transformation, you'll continue bleeding time on manual processes, losing trust through communication gaps, and watching customers move to more efficient suppliers.

If you embrace digital tools thoughtfully, you'll gain operational speed, business transparency, and customer loyalty that creates sustainable competitive advantages.

The reality is straightforward: today, digital isn't an optional upgrade; it's essential for survival. Digital tools don't just save time and reduce errors; they also create visible trust, enable consistent FAST execution, and strengthen every aspect of the BS Process.

This digital foundation becomes even more important as we move into the next chapter on Sustainability & Compliance. Because once digital systems build operational excellence, they also open doors to ESG compliance requirements, premium buyer relationships, and long-term partnerships that value responsible business practices alongside competitive pricing.

CHAPTER 11

Sustainability & Compliance

In the last chapter, we discussed how digital tools make the FAST Framework executable in daily operations. But technology alone isn't enough to stay competitive in today's evolving steel market. The next major challenge and opportunity for steel traders is sustainability.

This shift is happening because the world is asking tougher questions about every business:

- Where is your steel actually coming from?
- Is it safe, properly certified, and produced responsibly?
- Are your business practices transparent and ethical?

This is where sustainability becomes important as a business differentiator that separates forward-thinking traders from those who get left behind.

What Does Sustainability Mean in Steel Trading?

When most traders hear "sustainability," they immediately think:

- Expensive certifications.
- Complicated paperwork.
- And additional costs that don't seem to generate direct revenue.

I used to think the same way until I realized how much business we were actually losing by not understanding what sustainability really means in practical terms.

Sustainability sounds complicated, but at its core, it simply means doing business in a way that doesn't harm the future: your future, your customers' future, and the community's future.

This breaks down into three practical areas that every trader can understand and implement:

Environmental responsibility: Reduce waste in your operations, save energy wherever possible, and lower the carbon footprint1 of your business activities.

Social responsibility: Protect your workers' safety, ensure fair wages, and support the communities where you operate.

Good governance: Follow all applicable laws, maintain complete transparency in dealings, and avoid shortcuts that create long-term risks.

Together, these form what's called ESG standards: Environmental, Social, and Governance, which is essentially a simple checklist of whether your business operates responsibly.

Why We Need Sustainability

Many traders still think sustainability is just about looking good in corporate presentations or satisfying government requirements. But after working with institutional buyers and large developers, I've learned that sustainability directly impacts your ability to compete for the best contracts and build lasting relationships.

Sustainability isn't just about being a good corporate citizen; it directly supports and strengthens every pillar of the FAST Framework we've been building.

Here's how sustainability connects to practical business operations:

Frequency benefits from smooth approvals because compliance reduces delays and bureaucratic obstacles that slow down operations.

Availability depends on BIS-certified, reliable stock that customers can trust and projects can approve without additional verification.

Savings come naturally from energy efficiency improvements and waste reduction practices that cut operational costs.

Time improves significantly when paperwork, certifications, and compliance requirements are already in place instead of scrambling to meet them during urgent deals.

The consequences of ignoring sustainability are becoming expensive: risk of penalties and sudden project rejections, banks avoiding loans to non-compliant traders, and big developers choosing certified suppliers while leaving others behind.

But the benefits of embracing sustainability create competitive advantages: premium clients trust and prefer you, larger contracts become accessible, and long-term customer loyalty grows because you're seen as safe and stable.

Compliance as an Advantage

Many traders initially see compliance as just another expense and bureaucratic hurdle. New regulations can feel overwhelming, especially when you're already managing daily operations, customer demands, and market volatility. It's natural to focus on the immediate costs and paperwork rather than looking for potential business advantages.

Until recently, most of us treated compliance exactly that way, as pure overhead. Taxes, GST filings, BIS testing, and endless paperwork seemed like necessary evils that cost money without generating any revenue.

But something interesting has happened in the market. The business landscape has shifted, and now compliance actually opens doors instead of just costing money. What used to be just about avoiding trouble has become a way to win better contracts and build stronger relationships.

This shift happened because the market now actively rewards transparency and proper certification:

1. Banks offer better financing terms to businesses that maintain proper compliance records and demonstrate responsible operations.
2. Institutional buyers consistently prefer certified suppliers because it reduces their own risk and liability in large projects.
3. Major infrastructure projects like metro systems, smart cities, and industrial parks now shortlist only ESG-ready vendors from the beginning of the procurement process.
4. Compliance requirements are actually shrinking the grey market and creating more opportunities for transparent, well-documented businesses.

The irony is that what once felt like a burden has become one of the most reliable ways to stand out in a crowded market. Instead of just keeping you out of trouble, proper compliance now keeps you ahead of the competition.

Sustainability as a Differentiator

The steel market is changing in ways that many traditional traders haven't noticed yet.

- Customers are asking different questions.
- Projects have new requirements.
- And the definition of "quality" now includes factors beyond just tensile strength and chemical composition.

The steel products themselves are evolving toward sustainability. From rust-protected pipes that last longer to low-carbon TMT bars that reduce environmental impact, customers increasingly want materials that support their own sustainability goals.

When you adapt to this shift, instead of being just another supplier competing on price, you become a trusted partner helping customers build better, safer infrastructure.

The most successful businesses in any industry combine good profits with responsible practices; steel trading is no different.

Implementation Roadmap for Traders

One of the biggest mistakes I see traders make is thinking they need to become completely "green" overnight or invest lakhs in certifications before they can compete. This all-or-nothing thinking keeps many good traders stuck in old patterns while opportunities pass them by.

But you don't need to transform your entire business overnight. Sustainability can be built gradually through practical steps that fit your current resources and grow with your business.

Start with these fundamental compliance requirements:

Step 1: Master basic compliance. Ensure BIS certification for all products, maintain disciplined GST and tax filing, and provide lab testing reports for complete transparency.

Step 2: Add practical sustainability practices. Reduce material wastage through proper storage and careful handling, optimize truck loads to cut fuel consumption, use energy-efficient equipment in warehouses and offices, and ensure worker safety with protective gear and proper training.

Step 3: Invest according to your capacity. If the budget is limited, start with simple habits like better stock handling, paperless billing, and LED lighting. With a medium budget, add GPS tracking for fuel efficiency and rainwater harvesting. With a higher budget, consider solar power and advanced waste recycling systems.

Step 4: Get proper recognition. Progress from BIS Certification to ISO standards to full ESG reporting, then showcase these credentials in catalogs, WhatsApp updates, and pitch presentations to win larger contracts.

The beauty of this approach is that each step builds on the previous one, and every improvement, no matter how small, starts paying dividends immediately. You don't need to wait until you've completed all four steps to see benefits. Even basic compliance and simple efficiency improvements begin opening doors and saving money right away.

Decoding What Holds Traders Back!

When I discuss sustainability with other traders, they often raise practical concerns that deserve honest answers:

"Is this really necessary for local markets?"

Yes, because even local buyers now ask for BIS and quality certifications. Tomorrow, even small contractors will prefer compliant traders because it reduces their project risks and liability.

"But this costs money upfront."

True, but non-compliance costs far more through penalties, rejected orders, and missed opportunities. Trust backed by proper certifications becomes money in the bank.

"Isn't this too expensive for smaller traders?"

Actually, a BIS certificate costs less than the profit margin from a single medium-sized order. The ROI comes quickly, especially when institutional buyers become accessible.

Business Benefits of Sustainability

I've had traders tell me that sustainability sounds nice in theory, but they need to see real numbers before they'll invest time and money in changing how they operate. This skepticism makes sense; we're all running businesses, and every investment needs to show clear returns.

The financial benefits of sustainability are real and measurable, not just feel-good improvements that look good in marketing materials but don't impact your bottom line.

When you invest in proper certifications and responsible practices, the market rewards you in ways that traditional trading approaches simply can't match:

Higher profit margins become possible because premium clients willingly pay more for certified, reliable materials.

Access to bigger projects opens up opportunities in metro construction, airports, highways, and housing societies that shortlist only ESG-ready suppliers.

Better financing terms from banks that extend longer credit lines and offer lower interest rates to compliant businesses.

Reduced business risks eliminate fears of sudden government raids, penalty assessments, or compliance-related shutdowns.

Future-proofing ensures that when new regulations emerge, you'll already meet the requirements instead of scrambling to catch up.

I've seen traders invest a few lakhs in proper compliance and safety measures, then land institutional contracts worth crores that they never could have accessed before. The return on investment happens faster than most people expect, especially once you become eligible for the bigger opportunities.

The New Steel Equation

The old steel trading formula was simple: tonnes × price = revenue. But that's not enough anymore in today's market.

The new equation is:

Tonnes × Price × Responsibility = Sustainable Revenue and Growth.

Sustainability supports the FAST Framework by ensuring the smooth flow of materials, money, and customer trust. Compliance makes the BS Process more credible and future-proof against changing regulations. And ESG doesn't just mean checking boxes to satisfy auditors, it's to earn deeper loyalty, attract bigger clients, and build growth that lasts.

The choice is becoming clear: traders who treat sustainability as an unwanted cost will always be chasing thin margins and fighting for scraps. Traders who treat sustainability as a strategic investment will build businesses that command respect, premium pricing, and long-term partnerships.

In the next chapter, we'll explore how this transformation leads to an even bigger opportunity when traders stop being seen as mere middlemen and start becoming true Growth Partners in their customers' success stories

CHAPTER 12

From Trader to Growth Partner

The FAST framework taught that steel trading isn't just about tonnes and rates, it's about mastering Frequency, Availability, Savings, and Time. But FAST alone isn't the final destination. It's the foundation that makes everything else possible.

- Without FAST, you can't deliver consistency.
- Without consistency, you can't build trust.
- And without trust, you can't evolve into what the market really needs: a Growth Partner who drives success for everyone in the ecosystem.

Consider this: moving material frequently makes you reliable, guaranteeing availability builds loyalty, controlling costs allows you to reinvest in relationships, and respecting time earns repeat business.

Being a Growth Partner means carrying FAST into every interaction so that your role shifts from simply supplying steel to creating strategic impact for every stakeholder you work with.

From Middleman to Value Creator

For decades, steel traders played a straightforward role; they were the bridge connecting mills to buyers, taking orders and fulfilling them. But the most successful businesses today have moved far beyond that basic function. Instead of just moving steel from point A to point B, they create genuine value for everyone they work with.

This transformation shows up in practical ways that make a real difference:

1. Guiding builders on optimal sizes and grades that will work best for their specific projects and reduce waste.
2. Helping contractors plan logistics more efficiently so their projects stay on schedule and within budget.
3. Educating agents about price trends and market shifts so they can advise their clients better and close more deals.
4. Supporting suppliers with timely payments and steady demand that helps them plan production and maintain quality.

In short, a basic supplier just sells steel and moves on to the next transaction. A growth partner builds lasting trust that creates ongoing opportunities. And trust, once established, has a way of multiplying business in ways that pure price competition never can.

360° Relationships That Compound Growth

Real, sustainable growth never comes from individual deals or one-time transactions. It emerges from building an ecosystem of trust where every relationship strengthens the others. When you become genuinely valuable to all the key players in your market, growth stops being linear and starts compounding.

Here's how this ecosystem approach creates momentum:

Agents feel secure and confident when commissions are transparent, dispatches happen smoothly, and problems get solved quickly without drama or finger-pointing.

Developers sleep better at night knowing their projects won't stall because of material shortages or delivery delays that could cost them lakhs in penalties.

Suppliers appreciate working with someone who maintains discipline in payments and creates steady, predictable buying cycles that help them plan their own operations.

When all three types of relationships grow stronger together, every satisfied supplier recommendation leads to new opportunities. Every happy agent referral brings in better projects. Every loyal developer becomes a source of consistent, profitable business.

The success starts feeding on itself in ways that individual deal-making simply can't match.

Why Make This Shift?

Some traders look at the growth partner approach and wonder if it's worth the extra effort. Why not just stick with the simple buy-low, sell-high model and avoid all the relationship complexity?

Here's why this shift makes sense:

Premium pricing becomes possible when buyers willingly pay 25% higher margins for reliability and peace of mind rather than shopping purely on price.

Customer loyalty reaches 80% repeat business rates because clients stop looking for alternatives when they find someone they can truly count on.

Accelerated growth happens at 3x the rate of traditional traders because trust creates referrals, bigger contracts, and long-term partnerships that compound over time.

The bottom line is simple: trust isn't just a feel-good relationship-building. Trust is compounding capital that generates returns year after year. The initial investment in building these deeper relationships pays dividends that exceed the profits from individual transactions.

Building the Growth Partner Mindset

The transformation from trader to growth partner starts with asking different questions about your daily work and long-term success. Traditional thinking focuses on immediate transactions and short-term gains, but growth partner thinking focuses on long-term value creation for everyone involved.

Instead of measuring success by asking "How many tonnes did I sell today?" the growth partner mindset asks different questions:

- "How many partners grew stronger because of our work together today?"
- "How many projects moved faster and more smoothly because of the systems we've built?"
- "How many people's work became easier because we removed friction and solved problems proactively?"

This shift in thinking changes a trader from just another supplier competing on price into an indispensable partner that people want to work with.

The more you focus on solving problems for customers, suppliers, and agents, the more your own business naturally grows, not through aggressive selling, but through relationships where everyone benefits from your success.

The Choice That Defines Your Future

Steel Trading 4.0 represents a fundamental choice about how you want to build and run your business. It's not about selling more tonnes or fighting harder for better margins. It's about creating a role that's so valuable and well-integrated into your market that your presence accelerates the entire ecosystem around you.

This choice comes down to two very different paths. You can continue operating as a traditional trader, fighting for margins on every deal and competing primarily on price. Or you can evolve into a growth partner who creates new opportunities and builds markets rather than just participating in existing ones.

The future clearly belongs to growth partners who choose the second path. They're the ones who will thrive as markets become more sophisticated, customers become more demanding, and competition intensifies. They're building businesses that compound value over time rather than just extracting value from individual transactions.

The tools, frameworks, and mindset shifts we've covered throughout this journey provide everything needed to make this transformation successful.

The question now is whether you're ready to move beyond traditional trading and step into the role of growth partner that the market is waiting for.

Epilogue:
Beyond Steel, Towards Legacy

As I look back on the journey of writing this book, and more importantly, living the lessons inside it, one thought keeps coming to me: Steel trading was always supposed to be about tonnes, trucks, and turnover. But I've learned it's really about something completely different: trust, time, and truth.

For decades, our industry was built on the strength of a handshake. Then came the storm of compliance requirements, digital systems, and fierce competition that changed everything. Many traders fell behind and couldn't adapt to the new reality. Some managed to adjust and survive the changes. And a few actually grew stronger through the challenges.

What made the difference between those who fell behind and those who grew stronger? It wasn't luck or having the lowest prices. It was a mindset, built on three fundamental principles that guide every successful business.

- First is honesty, because in a business where crores change hands in minutes, one lie can collapse years of carefully built good will.
- Second is systems, because no person, however sharp or experienced, can carry the weight of hundreds of complex deals alone without proper processes.
- Third is relationships, because steel may be hard, but business is always human at its core.

I've watched traders win major contracts not because they offered the lowest prices, but because customers trusted them completely. I've seen projects delivered successfully not because we operated the largest plant, but because we maintained total transparency throughout the process. I've witnessed young agents grow into powerful, respected traders simply because they stayed consistent in their approach, even when business was slow, and patience was tested.

These experiences taught me that successful steel trading isn't about having all the answers from day one. It's about learning from each challenge and building systems that prevent the same problems from happening again.

A Hero Rises From The Challenges

The Birth of FAST

You might wonder how the FAST Framework actually came together. The truth is, it wasn't planned in a conference room or designed by outside consultants.

→ It emerged from real problems we faced every day in our business, solutions we developed through necessity, and lessons that sometimes hurt to learn.

→ The FAST Framework: Frequency, Availability, Savings, and Time, was born from years of trial and error, moments of genuine crisis, and insights that shaped how we think about this business.

➢ When dispatches were consistently delayed, and customers started losing confidence, we learned the critical value of FREQUENCY.

- When telling customers "not available" cost us important orders, we finally understood the power of AVAILABILITY.
- When invisible costs kept eating our margins despite strong sales, we discovered how much SAVINGS really matter.
- And when missed timings meant missed opportunities that never came back, we realized that TIME is the real currency of this business.

FAST wasn't developed as an academic theory or business school concept. It was a survival instinct, gradually refined and turned into a reliable system. Over time, that system became the foundation for sustainable growth that didn't depend on market luck or perfect timing.

Steel Trading 4.0 and Beyond

As Steel Trading 4.0 continues to evolve, I see a future where traders will no longer be judged only by tonnes sold or prices quoted. Success will be measured by completely different standards that reflect the changing expectations of modern business.

Future success will depend on how seamlessly traders can integrate digital tools into their daily operations without losing the personal touch that builds relationships. It will be measured by how responsibly they align their practices with sustainability requirements and compliance standards that customers increasingly demand.

Most importantly, it will be determined by how effectively they transform from being mere transaction facilitators into becoming genuine growth partners for developers, agents, and suppliers.

The future will belong to those who can successfully combine profitability with responsibility, systematic processes with personal sincerity, and advanced technology with old-fashioned trust. These aren't contradictory goals; they're complementary strengths that reinforce each other when done properly.

This book, then, isn't just about implementing Steel Trading 4.0 concepts. It represents a timeless truth that applies to any business built to last: genuine growth comes to those who commit to playing the long game instead of chasing quick wins.

My message to every trader, whether you're just starting out or have decades of experience, comes down to three simple principles that have guided my own journey.

1. **Build your business slowly and deliberately,** but always build it honestly without cutting corners that will hurt you later.
2. **Adopt modern systems and technology to stay competitive,** but never lose the personal touch that makes customers want to work with you specifically.
3. **Value profits and business success,** but never pursue them at the cost of the relationships that make long-term success possible.

Throughout this journey, I've been guided by a simple philosophy that my family taught me, which I am resharing here again, captured in a doha by the poet Kabir that has always stayed with me:

"साई इतना दीजिए, जामें कुटुंब समाय।
मैं भी भूखा न रहूँ, साधु न भूखा जाय॥"

"Give me enough, Lord, that I can care for my family, and still have something left to serve others."

This verse captures the spirit in which I hope you read these pages and apply these lessons. It reflects the spirit in which I have tried to live my own journey in this business. And it represents the spirit in which I believe steel trading will continue to grow stronger, not just as a way to make money, but as a way to build something meaningful that lasts.

If this book helps even one trader build a stronger, more sustainable business while staying true to these values, then every hour spent writing it will have been worthwhile. The steel industry has given me everything I have today. This book is my way of giving something back to the community that raised me and the traders who will shape its future.

Steel may be our business, but relationships are our legacy. Build both with care, and they will serve you well for decades to come.

— Ashish Agarwal

Founder, BS Group